SELF-EFFICACY: RAISING THE BAR FOR STUDENTS WITH LEARNING NEEDS

Joanne Eisenberger
Marcia Conti-D'Antonio
Robert Bertrando

EYE ON EDUCATION
6 DEPOT WAY WEST, SUITE 106
LARCHMONT, NY 10538
(914) 833–0551
(914) 833–0761 fax

Library of Congress Cataloging-in-Publication Data

Eisenberger, Joanne, 1942–
    Self efficacy: raising the bar for students with learning needs / by Joanne Eisenberger, Marcia Conti-D'Antonio, Robert Bertrando
        p.   cm.
    Includes bibliographical references.
    ISBN 1-993001-90-0
    1. Learning disabled children—Education—United States. 2. Inclusive education—United States. 3. Independent study—United States. I. Conti-D'Antonio, Marcia, 1953– II. Bertrando, Robert, 1941– III. Title.

    LC4705.C67 2000
    371.92′6—dc21

10 9 8 7 6 5 4 3 2 1

99-055007

Cover design by Carolyn H. Edlund
Editorial and production services provided by
Richard H. Adin Freelance Editorial Services
52 Oakwood Blvd., Poughkeepsie, NY 12603-4112
(914-471-3566)

Also Available from EYE ON EDUCATION

Supporting Students with Learning Needs in the Block
by Marcia Conti-D'Antonio, Joanne Eisenberger, and Robert Bertrando

**Making Decisions about Diverse Learners:
A Guide for Educators**
by Fern Aefsky

**Personalized Instruction:
Changing Classroom Practice**
by James Keefe and Jack Jenkins

**Working in a Legal and Regulatory Environment:
A Handbook for School Leaders**
by David Sperry

**The Administrator's Guide to
School-Community Relations**
by George Pawlas

**Educational Technology:
Best Practices from America's Middle Schools, 2d ed.**
by William Bozeman

Research on Educational Innovations, 2d ed.
by Arthur Ellis and Jeffery Fouts

School-to-Work
by Arnold Packer and Marion Pines

**Staff Development:
Practices That Promote Leadership
in Learning Communities**
by Sally Zepeda

**Transforming Schools into
Community Learning Centers**
by Steve R. Parson

**Urban School Leadership:
Issues and Strategies**
by Eugene Sanders

**The Educator's Brief Guide to the Internet
and the World Wide Web**
by Eugene F. Provenzo, Jr.

**What Schools Should Do to
Help Kids Stop Smoking**
by William Fibkins

**The Reflective Supervisor:
A Practical Guide for Educators**
by Ray Calabrese and Sally Zepeda

FOREWORD

We ask a lot from teachers. In truth, it cannot be any other way. Teachers are architects of lives. A human work-in-progress comes to school. Willingly or not, that child will spend the bulk of his or her prime waking hours in a classroom, working at the direction of a teacher.

The way in which that child experiences the classroom will contribute in important ways to whether the child hungers after learning or seeks to escape it, feels empowered or dehumanized, becomes part of a community of peers or is set apart from the group. There is great power in the role of a teacher and no teacher can avoid exercising it. What we *can* do as teachers is continually prepare ourselves for the wise use of the power that is unavoidably ours.

Teaching has never been easy. There have always been too many learners assigned to too few teachers. Learning spaces have always been too restrictive, materials too few. We have always been starved for time.

In addition, teachers encounter each day the most diverse student populations we have known. Students come from varied cultures which equip them with a wide array of lenses through which they view the classroom and life. Gender still shapes and separates us, with gender role variance compounding cultural and language variance. Some students come to us years ahead of the prescribed curriculum, while others are years behind it. Even advanced students may not excel in all areas, may do battle with emotional or behavioral demons, or may struggle with learning disabilities. And still, there are too many students, too few teachers, too little space and a dearth of time.

Excellence is a highly personal thing. To ensure each learner's access to personal excellence, we must come to understand how to meet each learner as he or she comes to us, and help that learner grow as far and as fast as possible. We need to help each learner extend and discover interests and talents. We must create environments that help each learner learn more about how to learn best.

Most of us will also need to develop a far richer reserve of strategies to help students develop the attitudes and skills of successful learning. We need not a hefty bag of tricks, but knowledge of what makes people successful. We must develop increased sensitivity to the great variety of impediments to personal and academic success. We need to figure out what stands between any student and the next increment of growth. We must also develop the skill to flexibly apply concrete strategies that help each learner exercise increased personal control of success.

We will also have to become much more comfortable with orchestrating multi-task classrooms with a consistent and purposeful mix of whole class, small group, and individual work; where time is flexible; and where learners share responsibility with the teacher for smooth functioning of the classroom.

Since so many of us have become skilled at teacher-led, whole group instruction, this challenge is a significant one.

The authors of this book offer pedagogy for academically diverse classrooms. They provide concrete models for supporting student success and help us understand the intent of the models so that we can develop some approaches of our own.

This book is important to me because it builds scaffolds, not excuses, for teachers and students alike. It challenges teachers to do what students must also do—maintain the belief that we can achieve complex goals, persist in working toward those goals, and be resilient when the day does not go well.

The book evokes images of classrooms in which teachers and students are fiercely determined to maximize the possibilities of every person in the room, where teachers and students are increasingly savvy about how to make that happen, and where both are willing to work long and hard when success seems most distant. That's what all our classrooms ought to be like. This book helps us move in that direction.

Carol Ann Tomlinson, Ed.D.
The University of Virginia

ABOUT THE AUTHORS

Joanne Eisenberger, has been in public education for 36 years. After two years in the Peace Corps in Liberia, she taught mainstreamed Special Education classes in Washington, California, New York, and Pennsylvania. She is currently 504 Coordinator in the Unionville-Chadds Ford School. A coauthor of *Supporting Students with Learning Needs in the Block,* she earned her Masters Degree in Special Education from San Francisco University.

Marcia Cont-D'Antonio is Director of Special Education for the Unionville-Chadds Ford School District. A coauthor of *Supporting Students with Learning Needs in the Block,* she has been in public education for 26 years with teaching experiences in elementary education and in special education K-12, as well as with the diagnosis of learning disabled students. She directed two federally funded projects to train educators to teach Special Education students included in their classrooms. She earned her Masters Degree in Special Education from Temple University and completed her graduate work in reading at University of Pennsylvania.

Robert Bertrando, a coauthor of *Supporting Students with Learning Needs in the Block*, is the social studies supervisor for the Unionville Chadds-Ford School District. He has been in the field of public education for 36 years, having begun his teaching career as an English/social studies teacher. He has been involved in designing and coordinating district initiatives to adapt curriculum and instruction to meet the needs of the diversified learner. He earned his B.A. from Pennsylvania State University and his masters degree from West Chester University.

PREFACE

Significant new changes have occurred in education. Both the Individuals with Disabilities Education Act (IDEA) and Section 504 of the Americans with Disabilities Act (ADA) have become the legal mandates that now force educators to examine and improve the way access is provided to a Free and Appropriate Education (FAPE) to all students. We wrote this book to assist the educational community in making appropriate responses to the requirements of IDEA. The changes have also forced educators to examine their practice and test the limits of how inclusion of special-needs students impacts teachers, administrators, and other students on a daily basis. IDEA will not go away. Its elements might be modified through the courts, but it will not disappear. Waiting, as educators sometimes do, "for this to pass," will not serve the professional community well. When elements of the law are tested in the courts, school districts must respond.

Although IDEA has its flaws, and opposition to elements of IDEA can be heard in school board chambers, teachers' lunchrooms, and taxpayer group meetings, there is one fact that can not be debated. Special education has become everyone's concern, and the line between special education and general education has been blurred.

The general educator is affected most acutely because students with learning needs are a part of the general curriculum and will be included in almost every classroom. The term inclusion is not contained in the law, but the term Least Restrictive Environment (LRE) is. The law states that:

> to the fullest extent appropriate, handicapped children, including those children in public and private institutions or other care facilities, are educated with children who are not handicapped, and that special classes, separate schooling, or other removal of handicapped children from the regular educational environment occurs only when the nature or severity of the handicap is such that the education in regular classes with the use of supplementary aids and services cannot be achieved satisfactorily (P.L. 94-142, Section 1412 [5] [B]).

The burden now falls on school districts to prove why a student should *not* be fully included. The most common types of relief sought, when bringing cases to trial, are *inclusion* and private school placement. Recent court cases are used to interpret the standard of LRE. The common features among the cases are:

+ An overriding determinant to educate disabled with nondisabled

+ A deference to locale authority

+ The willingness to measure the effect of disabled child on nondisabled peers

◆ A willingness to consider cost

Recently, even mainstream press has responded to IDEA and the requirement for "supplementary aids and services." Jon Leo's "Let's Lower the Bar" (1998), an article written for *US News and World Report*, cites a law student who exercised her right to accommodations and took the New York Bar exam five times using "double time" as an accommodation and scored 143 in a class of 153 students. He asks if such accommodations are forcing institutions to lower minimum standards. Tamar Lewin, in *Shaky Crutch for the Learning Disabled* (1998), reminds his readers that employers are not required to hire people who cannot meet the requirements of the job, but wonders what will happen to job performance when people with accommodations for their disabilities function in the workplace. In the same article, the reader is reminded that most handicapped people self-select tasks that they can handle and that successful people with handicaps succeed because they are often very motivated.

This book focuses on this note of motivation and on what is necessary for handicapped people to be successful. to achieve success, individuals must believe that they have the abilities needed to produce quality work through sustained effort. This definition of success is referred to throughout this book on self-efficacy. This book gives us an opportunity to take the good and positive elements that have been learned from the practitioners in the field of special education to enhance learning for all students. Change initiatives in special education parallel similar efforts in general education (Falvey, 1995). When school districts embrace initiatives that improve learning for all students, high standards and rigor for all students, and opportunities for self-efficacy, then meeting the needs of special education students will not be seen as a separate process but as part of the natural context for quality general education.

Educators currently in the field as well as those in preservice will benefit from this book. We refer to specific instructional strategies for self-efficacy throughout the book, as well as to authentic student artifacts that we used when teaching for efficacy. We believe it is critical to communicate clearly to parents about progress in the general curriculum as well as what supports efficacious behavior in children. We include valuable information for working together with parents toward this goal of independence. The appendix has ready-to-copy black-line masters of the forms and Curriculum-Based Assessments that we use in our classrooms. Using these will let you go right to work.

REFERENCES

Falvey, (1995). *Inclusive and Heterogeneous Schooling: Assessment, Curriculum, and Instruction.* Baltimore, MD: Paul H. Brookes.

Leo, J. (1998, October 5). Let's lower the bar. www.usnews.com (Outlook on Society).

Lewin, T. (1998, October 10). Shaky crutch for the learning disabled. *New York Times,* 1–5.

TABLE OF CONTENTS

Introducing Self-Efficacy

On March 12, 1999, the U.S. Department of Education announced the final regulations implementing the Individuals with Disabilities Education Act (IDEA) Amendments of 1997. As a result of these amendments, states must now include students with disabilities in their statewide and districtwide testing programs and include their scores in school reports. It is, therefore, incumbent on the states and school districts to provide disabled students with appropriate accommodations to participate in the assessment or to develop alternate assessments for those students who, even with accommodation, cannot participate. Some fear that by including the scores of the disabled students, norm-referenced achievement test scores will be lowered. If appropriate accommodations are made and appropriate alternative tests developed, the impact of the scores of the disabled students should be negligible. Unfortunately, some states forbid the use of appropriate accommodations and modifications in their state-mandated assessments. This mind-set demonstrates a total lack of understanding of the regulations and spirit of IDEA.

Similar concerns have been expressed about how the standards movement will make it more difficult for special education students to succeed in school. The standards movement poses no threat to students with disabilities. In fact, by establishing critical content and skill outcomes for students to know, understand, and be able to do, states have helped to define more clearly what is critical for students to master. However, it does little good to raise standards for all students if the curriculum does not contain the means by which children can achieve these elevated standards and if instruction is not able to meet the varied and unique needs of students.

The general education curriculum is a continuum of outcomes and skills for people 3 to 21 years old. It involves all of the activities, materials, instructional techniques, and objectives experienced by all students in the school. The general education curriculum concerns itself with processes as well as content outcomes. It is in the area of skills and processes that most school curricula seriously fall short in helping regular education students achieve, not to mention special education students. It is pointless to raise standards and not help students develop the skills, attitudes, and dispositions necessary to be successful, independent learners. These skills, attitudes, and dispositions build the belief that a person has the necessary abilities to produce quality work through sustained effort—self-efficacy.

Students must be given the tools necessary to succeed not only in school, but in life as well. To be a self-directed learner requires more than developing a set of learning skills and strategies. It requires the development of a self-efficacious attitude, which ultimately leads to an independent and responsible member of society—a goal that all schools profess to value. A school that strives to develop this attitude in its student body must offer a curricular cycle that provides students with opportunities to develop goal-setting strategies, planning strategies, strategy and skill development, and finally, an opportunity for reflection. The specifics of this Learning to Learn curriculum and how to deliver it are explained in Chapter 3. This recursive, curricular cycle, which most likely will occur in a learning support classroom, can be easily merged into the general education curriculum. "The most effective instructional practices for inclusion are often practices that are effective for all students to achieve their greatest potential" (Conti-D'Antonio, Bertrando, & Eisenberger, 1998).

Schools that truly wish to promote self-efficacy must be willing to reconsider some policies and practices that have been in effect for years. These policies include a lockstep sequence of instruction, ability grouping, competitive grading, and comparative evaluations. These practices need to be replaced with differentiated instruction, student evaluations based on rate of progress, and cooperative rather than competitive classroom structures. These instructional strategies must be adopted by teachers who hold high expectations for all students; set high standards of achievement; reward behaviors conducive to intellectual development; structure and conduct learning activities to ensure mastery; and view parents as partners and education as a shared responsibility. In addition to these instructional attitudes, special education teachers must also remediate students, prepare them to learn, and teach to accelerate learning so that the student can rejoin the general education program as quickly as possible. This approach is in sharp contrast to the exclusive tutorial approach that often results in a high level of student dependency.

Although the changes in instructional practices that have been advocated appear to require a monumental shift in attitude, the truth is that most of these practices evolve slowly over time, teacher to teacher, student to student, and parent to parent. Success breeds imitation. As more special education students exhibit self-efficacious behavior, general education teachers become interested in learning techniques that they can use in their own classrooms. As a result of this interest, cooperation between special education teachers and general education teachers increases, which further spread those practices producing more independent, responsible students (see Chapter 2).

REFERENCE

Conti-D'Antonio, M., Bertrando, R., & Eisenberger, J. (1998). *Supporting Students with Learning Needs in the Block*. Larchmont, NY: Eye On Education.

1

SELF-EFFICACY VERSUS SELF-ESTEEM

The 1997 reauthorization of the Individuals with Disabilities Act (IDEA) is driving a fundamental change in the nature and practice of education in the United States. Suddenly, the vast majority of students, with all types of disabilities and learning problems, are the responsibility of the general education teacher. IDEA places emphasis on two primary principles that have broad implications for both general and special education:

♦ Most students, including those with disabilities, are best educated with their nondisabled peers.

♦ Students with disabilities must have access to the same skills, concepts, and understandings as their nondisabled counterparts.

Although it does not specifically require inclusionary practices, the intent of the law is clear. Schools must use inclusionary practices for all students and make available a full continuum of services to insure that all students have a free and appropriate education (FAPE) in the least restrictive environment (LRE). Schools that have not practiced inclusion must do so. All teachers must expect high standards of performance from all students. General education teachers, who may be content experts, must expand their knowledge, lesson designs, instructional practice, and assessment methods to allow the disabled access to the curricula they are delivering. Progress, previously limited to summative evaluations and measured in factual objective tests, must be expanded to include formative assessments that measure growth over time within the general curriculum.

IDEA has also redefined the curriculum, expanding the traditional definition to include multiple opportunities for students to show what they know, understand, and can do. General education is now defined as a continuum of outcomes and skills for all students ages 3 to 21. Whereas specific content knowledge is still an integral part of all curricula, the requirements of inclusion expand the definition to include skills and processes as well as activities, materials, and instructional techniques. Teachers must now attend equally to content and process and be able to articulate both. General education teachers now join parents as central members of the individualized education planning (IEP) teams, using their knowledge of the curricular demands and requisites, to develop IEP goals for special education students and service agreements for students protected by Section 504 of the Americans with Disabilities Act (ADA).

Because of IDEA, students with learning needs may arrive in general education teachers' classrooms with deficiencies in the strategies that are important for academic and social functioning. Students with learning disabilities may not approach tasks with a plan of action nor be able to estimate accurately how much time a task will require. Some of these students may exhibit disorganized thinking and have problems in planning, organizing, and controlling their lives in academic and social settings. Their school performance, when compared with their ability, may be poor. This issue may be evidenced on report cards that are rife with Ds and Fs. The work that they do may be incomplete or of poor quality. They may attribute their lack of work to personal feelings, request adult intervention and "help" before making an attempt, or avoid tasks completely by treating teachers and other adults as enemies to fight. They often have no strategies for comprehending, retrieving, or using information. They may have a tendency to complete only work that is effortless and openly complain if work requires effort. They behave as though they have no influence over how they live their lives. These are students who have not developed self-efficacy, the belief that they have the abilities needed to produce quality work through sustained effort (Figure 1.1). Because these students approach difficult tasks without self-efficacy, they make very poor use of their capabilities. However, with strategy instruction, students can make better use of their abilities. The student response in Figure 1.1 illustrates the power of strategy instruction.

FIGURE 1.1. A STUDENT'S RESPONSE TO THE SAME QUESTION BEFORE AND AFTER STRATEGY INSTRUCTION

Directions: Explain how your learning styles and intelligence strengths affect your learning.

Before Strategy Training

I think I learn better with groups because then I'm not depended on to do the whole project by myself. If I have a project I can fall back on my friends if I don't understand or need help, they would have the same topic.

After Strategy Training

I am a visual learner. I believe that by highlighting, keeping assignments & tracking my graids I will remember the things & that by positive self talk, having a studdie partner, and requesting for help on tests I will become a better learner.

A number of general education students also evidence learning or behavior problems that call for specialized or remedial instruction to develop a sense of efficacy. Because these students have not developed a belief in the learning efficacy needed to activate and sustain the effort and thought required for skill development, many of these students are at risk for school failure. These students can be informally categorized according to the causes of learning interference. These categories include students who exhibit cultural differences, slow learning rate, and underachievement, as well as students with diagnosed learning weaknesses or attention deficit hyperactivity disorders, and students who exhibit cumulative deficits or educational deprivation. Varied experiential backgrounds and/or inappropriate teaching, accompanied by some learning differences and weaknesses, account for the academic difficulties of these students. Without appropriate attention, these students eventually may become classified as exceptional and enter burgeoning special education programs.

Another important change brought about by the reauthorization of IDEA is the role the parent or guardian may play in planning for the education of their children. Although parents have traditionally been strong advocates for educating their children in the mainstream and an integral part of the educational process, the new regulations have further strengthened their positions. The IEP meeting must now be held at the parent's convenience, and parents are equal partners in the creation of the plans. Because of the strengthened position of parents, special education and general education teachers need to help parents recognize that the goal of IDEA is to graduate productive, independent citizens. Educators need to include parents in problem solving and goal setting so that efficacy training and reinforcement can occur at home as well as at school. Teachers need to articulate to parents the benefits of efficacious behaviors, provide concrete and accurate information about their children's progress, and be prepared to encounter opposition from parents and administrators as students who are accustomed to an "easy ride" express their complaints. Parents must also be supported as they struggle with the realization that appropriate but rigorous and demanding tasks need to be part of their child's education. For more information on working with parents, see Chapter 5.

IDEA has also redefined the role of the learning support teacher. Learning support teachers must expand their knowledge and instructional practices so that they can teach their students and share their expertise with fellow educators about how all students can be successful in general education classes. The learning support teacher must move away from a focus on tutorial to a focus on teaching for independence. Because their students will be educated in general education classes, learning support teachers must develop cooperative planning and cooperative teaching skills to support general education teachers as they struggle to be successful with students with learning needs.

Many programs for students with learning needs have unwittingly contributed to the low efficacy of these students by responding too quickly with help that rescues instead of teaches and with excuses that remove accountability. These practices are justified in the name of "self-esteem" when the effect of this behavior is to reinforce the student's sense of incompetence. The educators in these programs sometimes judge their success or failure with students by how happy and cooperative the student is. They attribute their lack of success with a particular student to "unfair" or "inappropriate" demands of the general curriculum or of a particular teacher. With the best of intentions, some teachers and guidance counselors protect and enable students, allowing the student to avoid using the persistence and effort needed to do well in school and life. The teachers spend most of their instructional time "helping" students complete homework and cram for tests instead of instructing students in the strategies needed for independence. These teachers openly justify their behavior by explaining how the student "feels," unwittingly reinforcing feelings of temporary happiness, long-term inadequacy, and an unacceptably high level of student dependency.

Responsible inclusion requires a continuum of service for students with special needs. Some students must be taught how to face gaps in their knowledge, skills, and competencies and be given experience with guided mastery to manage school. Support teachers may still need to teach some students in small groups outside the content classroom to meet their unique needs. However, the focus of these groups can no longer be tutorial. If students are to succeed in inclusive schools and enter society as independent adults, the support teachers must see their role as teaching strategies necessary for independence. The benefits of such teaching strategies can be seen in the student response below (Figure 1.2). For more exercises that promote self-efficacy, see Chapter 3.

FIGURE 1.2. A STUDENT IDENTIFIES NEEDED STRATEGIES[1]

Directions: Pick two strategies to learn and tell why you need them.

Strategy #1 <u>chairs in place</u>

I will use this for: <u>chairs in place sounds like a good idea for taking tests. I realize that I need to sit alone when taking a test.</u>

Strategy #2 <u>pocket process</u>

I will use this for: <u>I have problems paying attention so that's why I picked pocket process so I can get back on track. I can't sit and not wonder off in la la land.</u>

Some general education teachers are also unwitting partners in reinforcing poor performance by failing to hold students accountable or by using teaching practices that enable themselves to assume responsibilities that are really the students. General education teachers often avoid confronting the students, especially students with aggressive parents, and accept passive participation. The general education teachers, like the special education teachers, ignore behaviors that encourage low effort. Many of these behaviors were pointed out by Landfried (1989):

- ◆ Enabling students to "tune out" while the teacher does the talking and the thinking
- ◆ Consistently accepting "forgotten" assignments late or incomplete
- ◆ Giving credit for sloppy or partially finished work
- ◆ Ignoring cheating
- ◆ Enabling students who have not completed the basic work to pass courses with "extra credit"
- ◆ Giving easy tests and grades that require little of no serious effort or study
- ◆ Accepting excuses from students (I had to work late last night), which avoid accountability

---

1 For explanations of Chairs In Place and Pocket Process, see Appendix I: Strategies.

◆ Accepting excuses for poor performance from students with learning needs that would not be acceptable for the rest of the school population

◆ Consistently accepting and explaining away discourtesy from students because of learning needs

Some of this confusion and enabling behavior comes from a mistaken understanding of the role of self-esteem and self-efficacy. Robert Sternberg (1989) makes the distinction clear: When students essentially do tasks they originally thought to be too difficult they become more self-efficacious. It is a different quality that self-esteem which allows students to feel good about themselves with no basis in growth (Sternberg, 1989). In fact, students may judge themselves inefficacious in a task without suffering any loss of self-esteem because they do not invest their self-worth in the activity (Bandura, 1997). People may also be extremely efficacious but take no pride in their performance. Students who place a high value on social activities are not devastated by report cards that have Ds and Cs if they have consciously chosen to spend more time on social activities than on school. Neither a student's self-esteem nor self-efficacy is boosted by an "easy" A.

Performance attainment, a necessary skill for school success, is the product of self-disciplined effort. Well-meaning teachers confuse the lack of performance attainment with self-esteem. When this confusion arises, students' poor performance is attributed to a lack of self-esteem, when, in many cases, students actually lack self-efficacy (Figure 1.3). These students have an inaccurate judgment of their personal capabilities, an inability to regulate and monitor their application of skills and knowledge, and inadequate goal achievement.

FIGURE 1.3. THE CHARACTERISTICS OF SELF-ESTEEM AND SELF-EFFICACY ARE COMPARED

Self-Esteem	*Self-Efficacy*
Judgment of self-worth	Judgment of personal capabilities
Regulates happiness	Regulates acquisition of knowledge and skills
Self-liking	Self-discipline
Personal accomplishments	Performance attainment
Predicts satisfaction	Predicts effort and motivation
Product of social evaluation	Product of reflection
Produces contentment	Produces goal achievement

In a fully inclusive school, the special education teachers must build resilience and efficacy in their students. Students who are participating fully in academic programs, and for whom full participation in society is planned, must be able to apply what they know consistently and persistently, especially when academic progress is not going well. Building this efficacy requires that students experience overcoming obstacles through effort. Difficulties and setbacks actually serve a beneficial purpose. The struggle to overcome the obstacles teaches students that success usually requires sustained effort. If students with learning needs continually experience easy success, they come to expect quick results and are easily discouraged by failure. They give up quickly when faced with the smallest challenge. For academic success, teaching resilience is more important than modeling of strategies, cognitive coaching, or tutorial instruction.

Instruction in strategies and practice in applying the strategies will not improve academic achievement. However, reminding and reinforcing students for exercising better control over academic tasks by using the strategies will improve performance (Bandura, 1997). In other words, the more the learning support teacher can enhance students' beliefs in their ability to exercise control over academic progress, the better the academic performance. Therefore, the most important role for the learning support and the general education teacher is to provide the student with the rules and strategies needed to exercise control and to reinforce their students in applying the strategies for achieving their learning goals consistently and persistently.

Support programs and classroom remediation for students who fall behind should be designed to accelerate learning so students can make up deficits or learn the bypass strategies needed to rejoin the regular instructional life of the school. The student's progress should be closely monitored with quick corrective feedback given. The focus of the remediation or support should be to encourage the student to manage the his or her own learning and to become self-directed. For more information of the skills and strategies needed for academic success, see Chapter 4.

Experiencing success is an integral part of the process of building a strong sense of efficacy. Success builds personal efficacy, and failure undermines it. This is especially true if failure occurs before a sense of efficacy is firmly established (Bandura, 1997). Learning support teachers must, therefore, work closely with general education teachers during cooperative planning and cooperative teaching times. Working with content teachers to differentiate content, activities, and products in the content classroom to maximize the student's opportunity for success must become part of the learning support teacher's job. Learning support teachers must share their knowledge of students' strengths and weaknesses with the general education teachers so that differentiated assignments, based on interest, readiness, or learning profile can allow all students to maximize success while reinforcing a strong sense of self-efficacy. Exercises that enable students to make use of acquired skills, and demand high-level quality thinking and persistence must be developed (Costa, 1985).

Even when teachers have attended to the diverse needs of the class by constructing lessons, tests, and other curriculum-based assessments with extreme care, students with serious learning needs require additional accommodations or modifications to demonstrate mastery of knowledge and skills. But the accommodations must be carefully constructed and appropriate to avoid undermining a developing sense of efficacy. IEP teams should make accommodations, however, only when clear, objective evidence of need has been gathered from a variety of sources. These sources should include a variety of classroom observations, as well as standard, teacher-made, and curriculum-based assessments. The student's successful strategies and accommodations in Figure 1.4 are an example of how a student's observed needs can suggest appropriate accommodations.

**FIGURE 1.4. A STUDENT'S ACCOMMODATIONS
ARE IDENTIFIED BY LEARNING NEEDS[2]**

Name _Paul Jones_ Date _9/12/99_ Disability _Auditory Processing/ADHD_

My Academic Strengths	*Successful Strategies*
Short-term Visual Memory	3-Fold Page, 2-Column Notes
Verbal Reasoning	Study Partner, Stop and Think
Visual Processing Speech (in gifted range)	Muscle Reading, Graphic Organizers

My Learning Needs	*Successful Accommodations*
Auditory Processing	Visual Format for Information, Directions
Impulsive	Firm Limits and Boundaries—Avoid Verbal Debates
Task Completion	School-Home Communication
Attention and Concentration	Proximity, Goal Setting, and Reflection on Progress

---

It is also critical to understand that the need for any particular accommodation can change over time. As a student matures or learns new skills, a particular accommodation may no longer be appropriate. As the student learns and uses strategies that bypass weaknesses, a particular accommodation may need to be adjusted. An accommodation may be necessary and appropriate in one

---

2 For copies of the strategies mentioned in the Accommodations, see Appendix I: Strategies. A reproducible copy of the Accommodations form is located in Appendix II: Forms.

discipline but not in another. Because of the shifting nature of the accommodations, it is critical that special education teachers and general education teachers talk regularly and plan together.

Accommodations and modifications should never be used as a replacement for the time and energy students need to put into learning. Cooperating teachers who administer accommodations must be careful to avoid "helping" students to the point of cheating. Providing accommodations and modifications that reduce a student's opportunities to build the skills needed for successful actions teaches dependence and passivity while reinforcing low efficacy.

Accommodations and modifications are only appropriate if they do not invalidate the skill being taught or measured. Applying accommodations or modifications inappropriately can actually cause intellectual self-doubt and prevent students from putting enough effort into academic activities. This can severely undermine a student's accurate appraisal of the time, effort, and resources needed for academic success (Bandura, 1997). Appropriately designed accommodations and modifications can increase self-efficacy by allowing a student to act on a sound appraisal of his personal capabilities and increase the prospect of success.

All professionals must walk a fine line between keeping expectations for performance high, but reasonable, without providing so much "help" that the student is crippled by enabling behavior from adults (Conti-D'Antonio, Bertrando, & Eisenberger, 1998). The overriding message, especially for students who require accommodations and modifications, should be enablement. For more information on accommodations and modifications, see Chapter 4.

Developing student efficacy is largely dependent on the teachers' belief that they can be successful with difficult students. This belief translates into the way the teachers construct their lessons, their methods of delivering instructions, and how they maintain order and control. Efficacious teachers know how to prevent disruption from occurring by establishing the classroom as learning communities in which all styles and intelligence are honored. They maintain clear expectations, provide consistent structure, and sustain routine rules. These educators praise students for growth even when the growth is in small increments, and they deal with inappropriate behavior quickly and firmly. Figure 1.5 compares descriptors of lessons prepared by teachers with high and low instructional efficacy.

FIGURE 1.5. COMPARING INSTRUCTIONAL EFFICACY

Teachers with High Instructional Efficacy	*Teacher with Low Instructional Efficacy*
Believe all students are teachable	Give up quickly on students
Expect learning to require sustained effort	Create engaging but not effective, fun tasks
Teach appropriate strategies	Focus on dispensation of facts
Provide feedback and praise	Criticize and point out failures
Use persuasion, rigor, and intrinsic interests	Use coercive, punitive, and negative sanctions
Focus on student development	Focus on subject matter
Emphasize mastery experiences	Emphasize control and regulation

The more instructional support and help that teachers receive in managing their educational activities, the better their sense of instructional efficacy is. Schools that support and enhance teachers' self-efficacy have specific characteristics. These characteristics augment the teachers' sense of instructional efficacy, which is then transferred through interaction with the students. Teachers who are efficacious work in schools that possess these characteristics:

♦ Strong academic leadership
♦ High academic standards with learning activities structured and conducted in ways to ensure mastery
♦ Firm belief in student capabilities
♦ Partnerships of mutual trust, understanding, and respect between administrators and each other
♦ Sensitivity and respect for learning and teaching differences
♦ A collective sense of responsibility
♦ Structures that allow for problem solving versus assigning blame
♦ Systems that provide practical courses of action
♦ Power that is shared without undermining authority
♦ Systems of communication designed to inform and educate parents (Bandura, 1997)

School should be the place where all children learn the self-regulatory skills needed to manage their learning—places where children develop both the knowledge and the problem-solving skills needed for participating effectively in society. A strong sense of efficacy maintains the intrinsic interest and high levels of motivation that students need for such academic accomplishment and eventual autonomy.

REFERENCES

Bandura, A. (1997). *Self-Efficacy: The Exercise of Control.* New York: W. H. Freeman.

Conti-D'Antonio, M., Bertrando, R., & Eisenberger, J. (1998). *Supporting Students with Learning Needs in the Block.* Larchmont, NY: Eye On Education.

Costa, A. L. (1985). *Developing Minds: A Resource Book for Teaching Thinking.* Alexandria, VA: Association for Supervision and Curriculum Development.

Kouin, G. (1970). Discipline and group management in classrooms. In Brophy, J. (Ed.), *Teaching Problem Students.* New York: Holt, Rinehart & Winston, 1996, 10–11.

Landfried, S. E. (1989). "Enabling" undermines responsibility in students. *Education Leadership, 47,* 79–83.

Rimm, S. B. (1997). An underachievement epidemic. *Education Leadership, 54,* 18–22.

Sternberg, R. (1988). *The Triarchic Mind: A New Theory of Human Intelligence.* New York: Viking Press.

2

INSTRUCTING FOR SELF-EFFICACY

Strategy
Instruction

Differentiated
Instruction

Behavior
Management

Individuals with Disabilities Act (IDEA) has mandated that all students, including those with disabilities and learning problems, be educated to the greatest extent possible in the general education curriculum. IDEA has also broadened the scope of the curriculum beyond content knowledge to include processes and progress. The politicians, parents, and teachers who supported the passing of IDEA have reconfirmed the basic democratic nature, purpose, and benefits of public education:

♦ To support the development of a national identity among a diverse population

♦ To build the capacity for individuals to contribute individually and collectively to the economic well-being of the nation

♦ To create a literate citizenry that is capable of participating meaningfully and responsibly in a democratic society

♦ To provide a strong general knowledge base and the skills necessary to continue learning

Although the intentions of IDEA are laudable, the reality is that many general education and special education teachers are struggling with the new instructional role that has been thrust upon them. Special education teachers, many of whom spend most of their teaching time providing tutorial instruction, are struggling to redefine their purpose and to learn how to be successful with students who are being educated in the general curriculum. General education teachers, accustomed to delivering content, are now faced with educating students who have difficulty processing, representing, organizing, and retrieving information. If both groups of teachers are going to be successful, instruction must change, and a paradigm shift in what needs to be taught, as well as how a curriculum is taught, must occur.

A PARADIGM SHIFT

Consider the continuum of teacher views toward students and the actions taken by them based on those views shown in Figure 2.1. Educators' personal beliefs play a critical role in influencing student achievement and can be enabling or empowering, but not usually both. If students with learning needs are to be successful, teachers must make an effort to move their view of students toward the right on the continuum.

**FIGURE 2.1. THE CONTINUUM OF TEACHER
VIEWS FROM ENABLING TO EMPOWERING**

Enabling ⟵——————————————————⟶ *Empowering*

Students "need" the special education teacher if they are to be successful	Students are capable of growth through short-term intervention and return to the mainstream
The goal is for students to pass courses with Cs or better	The goal is for students to share decision making and responsibility with the teacher
Students receive short-term subject area tutoring designed to pass the next evaluation	Students receive instruction in strategies that transfers into all areas of school and the real world
Students depend on the system or the teacher and will fail without them	Students can become independent and will need less support in the future
Students need protection and rescue from the demands of academia	Students need to reflect on their thinking or actions to affect positive change

---

The strategy instruction required to increase efficacy and achievement in students with learning needs is intense and time consuming (Hughes, 1999). It is much easier for teachers to engage in short-term "feel good" tutorials or to deliver "help" that borders on cheating when administering tests. This practice serves no one well because it has very little lasting impact on the student's current behavior and often ensures dependence on the people doing the "helping."

For special education teachers, the shift must be away from tutorial as the sole function of special education classes. Special education teachers must expand their job to include teaching their students the self-efficacy skills needed to be independent learners. While supporting students in their general education courses, special education teachers must teach their students to apply what they know consistently, persistently, and skillfully, especially when the going gets tough and the stakes are high (Bandura, 1997). Both special education and general education teachers need to recognize and respect the notion that children who have deficiencies need large amounts of persuasion and positive experiences to overcome doubts about their ability and capacities.

The shift for general education teachers must be toward delivering a curriculum that includes instruction in the skills necessary for self-direction. Content instruction alone no longer suffices. General education teachers need to analyze existing curriculum to determine what tasks are worth having students spend time on and think about as they integrate the national and state standards. In other words, they must determine what in their courses are worth remembering, understanding thoroughly, and transferring to other areas. To be most successful with the wide variety of learning needs and nontraditional learners in all classrooms, general education teachers must now include instruction in the processes and strategies needed for independence such as those outlined by Bandura (1997):

◆ Instruction in the skills needed for planning, organizing, and managing activities

◆ Instruction in the skills needed for enlisting help and resources at appropriate times

◆ Instruction in the skills needed for regulating one's own motivation and to sustain involvement in activities

◆ Instruction in the skills needed for applying metacognitive knowledge and strategies for task completion

◆ Instruction in the skills needed for acquisition of the knowledge and skill for managing the environment

Special education and the general education teachers need to cooperate to develop criteria that can be used to measure performance with the focus on proximal learning goals and progress rather than products alone. Both groups must also develop multiple ways for students to show what they know, can do, and understand as well as provide students with feedback that rewards and reinforces performance. All educators must also understand that intellectual self doubts often plague special education students and prevent them from putting enough effort into academic activities. (For more information on assessing student progress, see Chapter 4.)

DIFFERENTIATED INSTRUCTION

The mandate of inclusion means that teachers must differentiate instruction to optimize learning for all students. Differentiated Instruction, developed by Carol Ann Tomlinson (1999), is a highly effective instructional framework for meeting the needs of a wide variety of students. In a differentiated classroom, general education teachers recognize and accept that students learn in different ways and at different rates, have different interests and different talents, and bring different life experiences with them. They plan for student similarities and student differences by carefully identifying the essential concepts, principles, and skills of their curriculum and by carefully constructing rigorous, but engaging, instruction that promotes a high degree of self-efficacy.

Differentiating Instruction is the process of varying the content the students are learning, the activities the students are engaged in, or the products students produce. This differentiation is further extended by considering students' readiness to learn, their level of interest in the material being explored, or the students' learning style or intelligence strength preferences. Instead of teaching to the middle, teachers who use Differentiating Instruction design multiple paths to learning and multiple ways for students to show what they know, understand, and can do. Differentiating Instruction allows gifted students to accelerate through the course work or to work at a high level of abstraction. At the same time, students who struggle with academic demands find or are given appropriate entry points for learning. As a result of this differentiation, all students have the opportunity to learn as much and as deeply as they can without the anxiety of being bored because the task is too limiting or frustrated because the learning is too taxing.

Because students in a differentiated classroom are engaged in different tasks while learning the same objective, specific preparation may need to be done. Teachers can help prepare students for differentiation by paying specific attention to the following:

- ◆ Building Acceptance
  - Engage in class and team building
  - Use cooperative learning structures
  - Use flexible grouping
  - Develop a sense of community
  - Establish common learning goals
  - Plan for multiple intelligence and learning styles
- ◆ Establishing Safety and Order
  - Articulate classroom rules clearly
  - Keep materials organized and easily accessible
  - Explain expectations clearly
  - Build in a tolerance for error and questions
  - Create and deliver instructions carefully
  - Engage students in talking about procedures
- ◆ Planning for correction and instruction so that each student gains competence
  - Activate Prior Knowledge
  - Provide a way to "fill in" knowledge gaps
  - Acknowledge small and large successes
  - Validate responses
  - Provide a way for students to get help
  - Keep parents informed

- ◆ Placing a High Value on Learning
  - Be enthusiastic
  - Keep all activity and product requirements rigorous
  - Teach learning strategies specifically
  - Have kid-watching tools prepared
  - Include both summative and formative evaluations
  - Make expected outcomes explicit
  - Give students responsibility for their own learning

A pyramid planner (Figure 2.2, p. 20) can ensure that consideration is given to the critical components of instructional design. The teacher can identify how the facts, concepts, and generalizations will be differentiated on the left side of the pyramid planner. The activities or processes that the students will engage in to construct for meaning can be listed on the right side of the planner. The teacher might also choose to differentiate the ways in which the student will demonstrate what they know, understand, or are able to do in the section of the pyramid planner labeled Products. To maximize efficacy training, specific learning strategies need to be embedded into content-rich lessons. Finally, the teacher must plan for both summative and formative assessment. The formative assessments will guide and inform subsequent instruction, and the summative measures will indicate the content and processes the students have learned.

Carol Ann Tomlinson (1999, p. 2) said it best:

> These teachers believe that all students should be held to high standards. They work diligently to ensure that struggling, advanced, and in-between students think and work harder than they meant to; achieve more then they thought they could; and come to believe that learning involves effort, risk, and personal triumph. These teachers also work to ensure that each student consistently experiences the reality that success is likely to follow hard work.

STRATEGY INSTRUCTION

Although incorporating ways to select, use, and monitor strategies for learning benefits all students, it is critical for nontraditional learners. Students with learning needs require the techniques, principles, or routines that enable them to solve problems and complete tasks independently. Teachers need to make the instruction of learning strategies part of their instructional scope and sequence if they are to be successful with students with learning needs. These students will need instruction in choosing the correct strategies, practice in applying the strategies, and reminders and reinforcements for exercising better control over academic tasks by using the strategies. The goal must be to enhance the students' belief in their self-efficacy, the ability to exercise control over academic progress. A new function of special education teachers is to work

---

FIGURE 2.2. A GRAPHIC ORGANIZER FOR
DIFFERENTIATING INSTRUCTION[1]

Pyramid Planner for Differentiating Instruction

Content (differentiated by Ⓡ I P ?)　　　**Activities** (differentiated by Ⓡ I P ?):

What SOME will learn: Use the algorithm $(A=L \times W)$ to find area	*Concrete—Using a sq. unit to find the area of various objects in the room.* *Representative—Create a visual represent-ation to prove a given # sentence.* *Abstract—Infer the formula from a graphic representation*

What MOST students will learn:

Use a graphic to explain the formula for area

Products (differentiated by R Ⓘ P ?):

Construct an illustration using polygons, angles & area.

Choose from: alien, underwater, sea animal, room in a house

What ALL students should learn:

Count area in sq. units

Identify angles: acute, obtuse & right angle

Identify polygons and their properties

Learning Strategies

Math attack

Think along

Requesting help

Teaching Strategies:　*Whole class and small Group (cooperative Learning buddies)*

Assessment:　*Observation on using Skills checklist, rubric for product*

1　For more information on the Learning Strategies mentioned below, see Appendix I: Strategies. A reproducible copy of the Pyramid Planner is located in Appendix II: Forms.

cooperatively with the general education teacher to identify those strategies that are critical for the student to meet the demands of the curriculum.

Special education teachers must recognize that students with learning needs will be more successful if the focus of support class is the explicit, structured teaching of learning strategies. The student response in Figure 2.3 illustrates that students also recognize the value of strategy instructions.

FIGURE 2.3. A STUDENT CHOOSES STRATEGY INSTRUCTION

In a recent discussion with Mrs. Conti-D'Antonio I made the decision to keep the every other day scheduling. This program is working well for me so far. My grades have improved a little bit and I feel more confident about school. Maybe in a future marking period I could maybe lessen my time and study more independently but for now I would like learn some more study skills and improve my grades up into the A and B range.

Because strategy instruction is intense and time-consuming, students need to know the rationale for the strategies they are being asked to use (Hughes, 1999). When a strategy has been taught to a student, the strategy must be maintained, practiced, and reflected on until it has become a part of the student's standard operating procedure. This requires substantially less time tutoring and much more time doing the following:

♦ Using diagnostic teaching—Being aware of the strategies the students are using, suggesting additional steps, teaching more efficient methods, making procedural corrections, or giving compliments

♦ Encouraging active learning—Requiring more prereading, prewriting, cooperative learning than the completing of homework

♦ Interrupting homework to provide as much practice and review of the strategies as possible—placing equal importance on process and product

♦ Pointing out and encouraging continued use and generalization of strategies

♦ Emphasizing the importance of automaticity of the strategies and basic skills as time savers

♦ Teaching students to monitor their own progress as they use the strategies—metacognitive awareness as well as automaticity are necessary for efficacy

♦ Reflecting on the success and the limitations of their strategies

Support teachers should be prepared to use a step-by-step approach to structure the initial steps in teaching a cognitive strategy. The process, Three Steps to Teaching Procedures, detailed by Harry and Rosemary Wong in *The First Day of School* (1998), is an ideal model.

1. **Explain.** State, explain, model, and demonstrate the procedure.

   Define the procedure in concrete terms.

   Demonstrate the procedures; don't just tell.

   Demonstrate a complex procedure step by step.

2. **Rehearse.** Rehearse and practice the procedure.

   Practice, step by step, under supervision and check for accuracy.

   Repeat the procedure until it seems routine.

3. **Reinforce.** Reteach, rehearse, practice, and reinforce the procedure until it is habit.

   Assess the automaticity and correctness of the procedure.

   Reteach any steps that are incorrect or unacceptable.

   Give corrective feedback.

   Praise the student when correction is made.

Because most of the lessons in a learning support classroom are individual, the best instruction occurs in short, less than 10-minute discussions with a student. The more the lesson can be compacted, the more powerful the message. The following four-step sequence is an effective model.

1. In 30 seconds or less, describe the issue. Use a Positive-Negative-Positive Feedback with "I message" format and end with a question. The teacher says, "You have such great potential and I am very concerned about your F in English. I would like to support you in your effort to get that grade up to passing. Can we plan together?"

2. Spend the next minute mirroring reality for the student. Provide an honest (but not brutal) overview of what has caused the problem. Do not use guilt or blame. Simply state the causes matter-of-factly and end with a question. The teacher says, "You have an F because you did not turn in the last three assignments. Can you share with me why you're are not doing the work?"

3. After listening to the student's explanation, spend the next two or three minutes teaching a strategy that will provide a solution for the student's dilemma. Make sure the strategy fits the subject and the student's learning style and will solve the problem if the student uses it. End with a question that asks for the student's commitment. The teacher says, "I have a suggestion for you. I want you to try to

use Hard to Easy for the next English assignment. This is what you need to do to use that strategy....Are you willing to try this for the next assignment?"

4. In 30 seconds or less, describe the payoff for the student (or ask the student to describe the payoff). The teacher says, "What will you have to give up to do this? What will you get?" Be positive, upbeat, and enthusiastic. Describe how the student will feel about the benefits of the strategy.

Because students with learning needs struggle to organize multiple tasks, both general teachers and special education teachers need to impose a "framework" that incorporates multiple strategies and give students enough guided practice in using the framework so that it becomes internalized and routine. Because students with learning needs do not spontaneously structure tasks and have difficulty activating specific strategies at appropriate times (Meltzer, 1993), substrategies and routines may also need to be taught. More information about specific strategies can be found in Appendix I. Academic progress is enhanced by instructional time devoted to teaching students how to develop solid, efficient learning plans. Time after completion of the activity for students to reflect on the effectiveness of their plans is also necessary.

One such framework is the Objective Test-Taking Cycle shown in Figure 2.4. The steps in the Objective Test-Taking Cycle provide visual, concrete guides to the multiple tasks needed to prepare for a test. The Cycle requires students to define how they will find and organize information; how they will shift from one strategy to the next and back again, if necessary; how they will monitor and check on their levels of readiness; and how they will evaluate the effectiveness of their chosen strategies when the test has been completed. Having a concrete model of the test preparation steps (Figure 2.5, p. 26) raises the level of awareness of the usefulness of strategies and illustrates the complex nature of test preparation.

A second framework that is important for students with learning needs involves the multiple mental tasks and skills that are needed to acquire information from written material. The process of extracting meaning from text combines several complex skills including reading comprehension, identifying key information and separating that information from examples and explanations, paraphrasing, and organizing information. The following framework is often called SQRRR, but Muscle Reading, a name coined by David Ellis (1991), is more descriptive of the effort needed to dig the key information from most texts and from some literature.

This framework (Figure 2.6, p. 27) gives a student a series of substrategies for extracting knowledge and information from extended passages in textbooks. This system works especially well for social studies and science texts because embedded language and dense information are the norm. At first, the system may seem awkward and cumbersome, and it takes time to learn and master. The payoff is a deeper understanding of written information, substantially less time rereading material, and a quality study guide to use in test preparation. If students are engaged in research, the same framework yields the notes needed to extract, organize, and synthesize the information needed to complete the project.

An additional framework involves using Graphic Organizers (Figure 2.7, p. 28) to coordinate the multiple tasks and skills needed to develop information-processing skills, demonstrate understanding of information, and organize written expression. The goal is to do what Edwin S. Ellis (1997) calls "Water Up" the curriculum so that all students have the effective and efficient strategies needed for meaningful learning. These graphic organizers allow students to construct knowledge instead of simply memorizing isolated facts. They allow students to understand the content by clarifying details and joining the details into meaningful wholes. They also make it possible for students to see how information falls into connected patterns and how the materials they are learning connects to their prior knowledge and experiences. Using the graphic organizers encourages elaboration in thought and writing and makes abstract information more concrete.

The final framework (Figure 2.8, p. 29) gives students a way to approach and organize the strategies needed for the successful completion of homework. This framework can be used to organize the strategies and the mental mind-set a student needs to complete the assigned work independently. Routinely using the Study Planner framework during class provides the guided practice in using the multiple tasks required for organizing time, materials, and attention students need on their journey to independence. General education teachers can also use the framework whenever their students are required to plan and work for a sustained period of time.

An additional benefit of the Study Planner is the opportunity it provides for the collection and recording of data about a student's progress toward self-efficacious behavior (see Figure 2.9, p. 30). Information noted on the Study Planner can guide instruction, provide a rich source of information for parent conferences, and form longitudinal study of a student's progress. For more information on working with parents and collecting data on student progress, see Chapters 4 and 5.

CLASSROOM MANAGEMENT

To be most effective, both Differentiated Instruction and Strategy Instruction should be conducted in classrooms where an efficacious environment has been established by teachers who have good behavior-management skills (Bandura, 1997). This environment is especially critical for nontraditional learners, many of whom act impulsively and have difficulty reading subtle social and environmental cues. Students who have learning needs require efficacious teachers who endorse high standards, backing them up with strong management

(Text continues on page 30.)

FIGURE 2.4. THE OBJECTIVE TEST-TAKING CYCLE[2]

Steps	*Possible Strategies*
❶ Set a Goal: Target a grade / Establish a time frame / Commit to strategies	Conferencing Journalizing Goal Pyramid / I Can Goal Visualization
❷ Identify Key Information	Graphic Organizer Cued Notes 3-Fold Page / Clustering Highlighting Cornell Notes / Math Assault Flashcards Post-Its / Color Coding Skimming Muscle Reading
❸ Memorize	Walk About Do & Redo Memory Webbing / Oral Research Peer Teacher Write then Read / Acronym Splashdown Key Word Pictures
❹ Check Memory: Recall the information / Keep track of # correct / Calculate your score	Practice Test Study Partner 3-Fold Page / Oral Retrieval Splashdown Flashcards / Walk About Computer Drill Cover & Recite
❺ Adjust Goal	Reward Yourself Goal Setting Accepting Feedback
❻ Repeat Steps 2, 3, 4	I will repeat: 1 2 3 4 5 times
❼ Take the Test	Visualization Splashdown Oral Retrieval / Eliminating Options Steal It Cued Notes / Chairs in Place Easy to Hard Using Margins
❽ Reflect on Performance	Reward Yourself Conclusions I Can / Test Critique Requesting Help Consequences
❾ Adjust Strategies	Responding to Persuasion Responding to Help / Decision Making Requesting Help
❿ Repeat the Cycle	Get a new Objective Test-Taking Cycle and begin preparing for the next test.

2 For more information on many of the strategies listed in the Objective Test-Taking Cycle, see Appendix I: Strategies. A reproducible copy of the Objective Test Taking Cycle is found in Appendix II: Forms.

FIGURE 2.5. A STUDENT USES A FRAMEWORK FOR CHOOSING, ORGANIZING, AND USING THE MULTIPLE STRATEGIES NEEDED FOR TEST PREPARATION[3]

Objective Test Preparation Planner

STEP	*STRATEGIES*
	Economics
1. Set a Goal	1. What grade are you willing to work for?
	A
2. Identify the Key Information	2. How will you separate out the facts that will be on the test?
	Cornell notes
3. Memorize the Information	3. How will you get the information into long-term memory?
	Oral Rehearsal
4. Check Memory	4. How will you find out if the facts are really in your memory and you can get them out of memory?
	Oral Quiz (partner)
5. Adjust Target Grade	5. How will you know if you can reach your original goal?
	By how much I know
6. Repeat Steps 3 to 5	6. How many times will you repeat Steps 3, 4, and 5 before the test?
	3 times, 1 each day before test
7. Take Test	7. What strategies will you use during the test?
	Stop and Think, Oral retrieval, Eliminate opt.
8. Critique Test Performance	8. How will you figure out what went right and what went wrong?
	By the Grade I received and what ?'s I misse.
9. Adjust Strategies	9. How will you prepare for your next test?
	The same way if it worked
10. Repeat the cycle	

---

3 For copies of the strategies mentioned by the student and a reproducible copy of the Objective Test Planner, see Appendix I: Strategies and Appendix II: Forms.

FIGURE 2.6. THE MUSCLE READING FRAMEWORK[4]		
Phase	*Steps*	*Possible Strategies*
Phase I Before you read (5 to 15 minutes)	1. **Preview**—Flip through the pages looking at section headings, picture captions, bold words. 2. **Warm-up**—Read the chapter review and the vocabulary list, identifying what you know. 3. **Notice**—Determine how the text is organized. 4. **Choose**—Select a note-taking strategy. 5. **Question**—Turn chapter headings and section titles into questions.	Prior Knowledge Request Help Decision Making Paraphrasing Study Partner
Phase II Reading & Writing (10 to 30 minutes)	1. **Read**—Use your questions to keep your focus and read aloud when your mind wanders. 2. **Visualize**—Picture the material in your mind. 3. **Take Notes**—Use the note-taking strategy selected. 4. **Answer**—Write the answers to the questions you asked yourself in the prereading phase. 5. **Expand**—Add details to your notes from class discussion and lectures. 6. **Predict**—Check your notes against what you think will be on the test. 7. **Question**—Write questions about what you don't understand and ask about those points in class.	Key Points Key Word Picture Graphic Organizer Post-Its Process 3-Fold Page Cornell Notes Outline Highlighting Flashcards Request Help

4 For descriptions of many of the strategies listed in the Muscle Reading Framework, see Appendix I: Strategies. A reproducible bookmark for students to use as a guide and reminder can be found in Appendix II: Forms.

Phase	*Steps*	*Possible Strategies*
Phase III After you read (5 to 10 minutes)	1. **Recite**—Talk to yourself about what you have learned, explaining as much as you can about each key point. 2. **Review**—Look at your notes within 24 hours of reading the material and fill in anything that you didn't understand. 3. **Check**—Practice retrieval to see what is already in your memory and what isn't. 4. **Review Again**—Review your notes once a day for about 5 minutes, reciting the more complicated information.	Oral Rehearsal Key Points Practice Test Oral Retrieval Cover & Recite Study Partner Do & Redo

FIGURE 2.7. GRAPHIC ORGANIZERS[5]

Function	*Graphic Organizers*
Construct Knowledge	Semantic Maps including Webs Debate Organizers
Clarifying/Connecting Details	Core Planning Charts Taba Charts Concept Clarifiers
Recognizing Patterns	Action-Reaction Charts Problem-Solving Structures Cause & Effect Diagrams
Elaboration	Multiparagraph Organizers

5   Two excellent sources of graphic organizers are Black, H., and Black, S. (1990), *Book 1 and Book 2—Organizing Thinking: Graphic Organizers*, Pacific Grove, CA: Midwest Publications, and Edwin Ellis (1999), *Using Graphic Organizers to Make Sense of the Curriculum*, Tuscaloosa, AL: Masterminds.

**FIGURE 2.8. A FRAMEWORK FOR LEARNING
TIME MANAGEMENT AND TASK COMPLETION**[6]

The Study Planner

Steps and Strategies	*The Plan*	

Before studying:
 	
Hard to Easy
Assignment Tracking
Materials Management
Personal Checklists
Chairs in Place
Goal Visualization
	I **organize** myself during the first 5 minutes by making a plan that clearly identifies my goal, subject, assignment, and strategy.
	
	   Goal: _____
	   Subject: _____
	   Assignment: _____
	   Strategy: _____
	
	I take responsibility for my **materials** by gathering all the supplies and equipment I need to complete the work I plan before I began.	

During the study session: Relax with Black Requesting Help Muscle Reading Stop and Think (Plus strategies specific to homework assignments)	I managed my **time** by beginning work at the time I have chosen. I show **commitment** by working the entire time I had planned, asking for assistance when I need information or instruction to complete my planned work. I actively participate in my own education by **completing** the work I planned so that I can achieve the goals I have established. I put myself back **on task** when distracted.	
After the study session: Rate yourself using the following key: I Can Accepting Feedback Smoke and Mirrors Stop and Think	**4 = Mastered** **3 = Good** **2 = Needs Work** **1 = Not Yet** **0 = Refuse**	I do this automatically. It is part of my school behavior. Even though I know this would help me be more successful, I still need to be reminded. I don't do this automatically. I know I should do this, but I often need to be reminded. I only do this when an adult suggests this or reminds me that it needs to be done. I only did this because I was forced to or because I was being watched. I refused to do this or I did not think this is necessary for me.

---

6 For descriptions of many of the strategies listed on the Study Planner, see Appendix I: Strategies. A reproducible copy of the Study Planner can be found in Appendix II: Forms.

FIGURE 2.9. A STUDENT PLANS FOR A 40-MINUTE CLASS AND A TEACHER RECORDS INFORMATION OF EFFICACIOUS BEHAVIOR[7]

Date 11/23 Period 5 Teacher E	SCORING:	Student	Teacher
Goal: _all goals_	1. Organize	4	4
	2. Responsibility	4	
Subject: _all subjects_	3. Materials	4	
Assignment: _Where are you now_	4. Commitment	4	
	5. Completing	4	
Strategy: _Conferencing_	6. Time	4	
	7. Feedback	4	
Assignment: _____	8. On Task	4	
Strategy: _____	9. Communicate	4	
	TOTAL:	100	

COMMENTS: _Complete goal & reflection & cleaned portfolios—_
Said he didn't do homework because he believed it was "too hard"

INSTRUCTION: _Requesting Help_

skills, and who provide, or at least cooperate with, support systems that aid mastery, and who believe that difficult students are teachable.

Good managers, those teachers who establish, maintain, and restore conditions that promote learning, have specific characteristics (Kounin, 1970). First, these teachers prevent disruption from occurring by providing effective environments and monitoring student behavior. Good managers do this by establishing standard operating procedures during the first weeks of school and then consistently maintain those procedures throughout the year. They establish routines quickly and clearly, and then monitor for compliance. Behaviors such as voice levels as well as rules about when to sharpen pencils and how to ask questions are observed, and consequences are consistently enforced.

Second, effective managers recognize and reward good behavior more often than they react to bad behavior. When it becomes necessary to punish, they do so with sadness and regret as though punishment is an unfortunate, necessary consequence of students' misbehavior but something that a student could avoid in the future if they wanted to do so. Teachers with strong instructional ef-

---

7 For more details on the strategies _Conferencing_ and _Requesting Help,_ see Appendix I: Strategies. For a reproducible copy of the study planner, see Appendix II: Forms.

ficacy tend to rely on persuasion instead of punitive measures and work toward the development of students' academic self-directedness.

Third, good managers minimize disruption by knowing when transitions will be difficult for students and by planning how to manage those transition times. They are keenly aware of who sits where and why. They plan the physical environment of their classroom so that it is most conducive to learning. They think through traffic patterns, determine where supplies will be kept so that traffic to and from those supplies is least disruptive, and they attend promptly to house-keeping chores. They recognize that most classroom disruptions can be prevented by diligently providing instruction that is rigorous, varied, and meets the needs of a wide variety of learners.

Kounin (1970) also identified four key behaviors that good managers use:

1. **With-It-Ness**—Continuously scanning the classroom, being aware of what is happening in all parts of the classroom, and intervening quickly and accurately before behaviors become disruptive by recognizing and responding to triggers.

2. **Overlapping**—Doing three or more things at once: responding to individual needs while sustaining the groups activities through the use of proximity, eye contact, or visual cues.

3. **Momentum & Continuity**—Developing compelling, well-paced lessons that are more attractive than the distractors.

4. **Challenge & Variety**—Maintaining effort through rigor and interest through differentiation.

Finally, good managers are aware that students with learning needs are not all alike and that different needs require different solutions. They are also aware that they do not have as much control over a student's behavior as they have over their own and that managing their own behavior will have a dramatic effect on the behavior of their students. The matrix in Figure 2.10 (pp. 32–36) is partially based on the work of Jere Brophy (1996) and Lynn Meltzer (1992) and identifies the teacher behavior that is most effective with individual problem types and the specific strategies that are most successful. Many of the strategies mentioned in the matrix can be found in the Appendix I: Strategies.

The goal of efficacious instruction should be the goal of inclusive schools —to teach the student the self-regulatory capabilities that enable the student to be reflective learners, capable of ongoing growth and persistence in the face of challenges.

(Text continues on page 36.)

**FIGURE 2.10. A LIST OF PROBLEM TYPES, INDICATORS FOR
ACCURATE IDENTIFICATION, APPROPRIATE TEACHER BEHAVIORS,
AND STRATEGIES THAT MAY NEED TO BE TAUGHT**[8]

Problem Student Type	Indicators	Teacher Behavior	Student Strategies
Flexibility disabilities: These children have difficulty shifting flexibly among different approaches. They may struggle to prioritize and to focus on salient details.	1. Difficulty adjusting to new teachers, situations 2. Talk around issues, cannot summarize 3. Poor study skills 4. Low reading comprehension	1. Scaffolding techniques 2. Clearly identify salient attributes of work 3. Sequenced, direct teaching of strategies 4. Environmental/physical cues for expected behavior	1. Strategies for rapid retrieval 2. Self-reflection strategies 3. Study routines: Math Assault, 5-day test prep, Muscle Reading 4. Summarizing strategies
Processing disabilities: These children process information slowly or in unique ways. They may be disorganized or use different processing routes to organize information. They show extremely strong learning style preference for one modality.	1. Discrepancies between class and test performance 2. Difficulty with timed tasks 3. Difficulty following directions 4. Written work, book bags are messy and disorganized 5. Often unprepared 6. Struggles to remember	1. Spiral or scaffolding instruction 2. Transfer cues 3. Require organization but not *one* method 4. Allow for extended time to organize, copy, process information	1. Semantic mapping, graphic organizers 2. Memorization strategies 3. Strategies that use strengths and bypass weaknesses 4. Self-checking strategies

---

8 For descriptions of many of the strategies listed in this matrix, see Appendix I: Strategies.

Problem Student Type	Indicators	Teacher Behavior	Student Strategies
Efficiency disabilities: These children do not finish assigned work. They do not monitor their work habits. They have difficulty coordinating the tasks needed to learn. They do not plan or check and begin work impulsively.	1. Slow to master strategies 2. Strong conceptual and reasoning skills 3. Cling to old habits 4. Inconsistent 5. "Careless" errors 6. "Lost" work	1. Coordinate multiple processes for student 2. Pace strategies used in close succession or simultaneously 3. Enforce consequences and reflect on causes	1. Organizational strategies 2. Planning and self-checking strategies 3. Goal setting and achievement 4. Strategies for directed attention (rubrics, ✔lists) 5. Bypass strategies and devices—calculator, referenced notes
Distractible: These children have short attention spans. They are unable to sustain attention and concentration. They are easily distracted by sounds, sights, movement.	1. Difficulty adjusting to change and transitions 2. Rarely completes tasks 3. Easily pulled off task 4. Moves or talks at inappropriate times	1. Environmental and instructional support 2. Reduce demands for sustained attention 3. Proximity and eye contact	1. Strategy to monitor and control attention—grade and assignment tracking, cross off as you go, attention tapes 2. Material and time management strategies 3. Carrels, behavior ✔lists
Low Achiever: These children have difficulty, even though they may be willing to work. Their problem is low potential or lack of readiness rather than poor motivation.	1. Difficulty following directions 2. Difficulty completing work 3. Poor retention 4. Progresses slowly 5. Poor abstract reasoning	1. Extra time, repetition 2. Place a high value on working hard, not happiness 3. Effort and progress are required 4. Work is acceptable as long as students apply themselves and are making progress in the general curriculum	1. Bypass strategies and devices—calculators, graphic organizers, spell checkers, guided notes, editing partners 2. Strategy more important than content—Muscle Reading, positive self talk, requesting help 3. Realistic self-assessment 4. Charting progress

Problem Student Type	Indicators	Teacher Behavior	Student Strategies
Defiant: These children resist authority and engage in power struggles with teacher. They want to have their way and not be told what to do.	1. Resists verbally—"You can't make me." 2. Derogatory statements about teacher to others 3. Resists nonverbally—looks away, frowns, laughs at inappropriate times, mimics teacher, deliberately does what the teacher says not to do	1. Ignore and avoid as much as possible 2. No powerful responses 3. Functional relationship 4. Environmental engineering	1. Professional counseling 2. Negotiated contracts 3. Strategies for responding to others
Passive-Aggressive: These children express opposition and resistance but not directly. Hard to tell if the resistance is deliberate. Often misdiagnosed as immature or attention seeking. Miscellaneous in form but exasperating in effect.	1. Subtly oppositional and stubborn 2. Controlling, borderline compliance with rules 3. Damages property—writes on desks, mars books 4. Disrupts surreptitiously 5. Drags feet	1. Recognize accurately, follow up with strategies 2. Offer support but refrain from doing for 3. Recognize anger but don't overreact to it	1. Problem-solving and problem-investigation strategies 2. Efficacious strategies—Requesting Help, Following Directions 3. Socialization strategies—Accepting Feedback, Conferencing
Immature: These children have poorly developed emotional stability, self-control, self-care abilities, and social skills.	1. Exhibits behavior associated with much younger children 2. Cries easily 3. Loses belongings 4. Frequently helpless, incompetent, and/or dependent	1. Emotional support but not low expectations 2. Cuing 3. Value on behavior changes	1. Self-determination strategies—Responding to Persuasion 2. Self-reflection strategies 3. Problem-solving strategies

Problem Student Type	Indicators	Teacher Behavior	Student Strategies
Failure Syndrome: These children are convinced that they cannot do the work. They often avoid starting or give up easily. They expect to fail, even after succeeding.	1. Easily frustrated 2. Give up easily 3. Says, "I can't do this."	1. Negotiated agreements 2. Specific proximal goals 3. Feedback stressing success 4. Efficacy training	1. Contracting 2. Goal setting with reflection 3. Coping strategies—test taking, memorizing, time management 4. Self-determination strategies—I Can, positive self-talk
Hostile-Aggressive: These children express hostility through direct, intense behaviors. They are not easily controlled.	1. Intimidates/threatens 2. Hits, damages property 3. Antagonizes, hostile 4. Easily angered	1. Avoid engagement 2. Enforce limits and consequences 3. Positive relationships	1. Professional help 2. Behavior management 3. Socialization strategies—accepting feedback, conferencing 4. Self-control strategies—dealing with frustration, managing anger
Peer rejected: These children seek peer interaction and acceptance but are rejected, ignored, or excluded.	1. Forced to work, play alone 2. Lack social skills 3. Picked on or teased	1. Positive group identity 2. Classroom as a learning community 3. "We…" statements	1. Socialization training 2. Strategies that target the undesirable trait
Shy-withdrawn: These children avoid personal interaction, are quiet and unobtrusive, and do not respond well to others.	1. Quiet and sober 2. Does not initiate or volunteer 3. Does not call attention to self	1. Expect slow change 2. Comfortable, secure classroom 3. Indirect pressure to change—invitation and encouragement 4. Cuing, shaping behavior 5. Environment engineering	1. Self-concept support—I can, eye contact. 2. Group projects 3. Study partners—Peer note takers, editing partners 4. Attention control strategies

Problem Student Type	Indicators	Teacher Behavior	Student Strategies
Perfectionist: These children are unduly anxious about making mistakes. Their self-imposed standards are unrealistically high, so that they are never satisfied with their work even when they should be.	1. Work must be perfect 2. Fearful/frustrated with the quality of the work 3. Holds back from class participation	1. Understanding, approval, and empathy 2. Honor motivation 3. Offer support to maximize achievement	1. Goal setting 2. Self-assessment 3. Diagnostic thinking—rubric for success 4. Realistic feedback
Underachiever: These children do a minimum to just "get by." They do not value schoolwork.	1. Indifferent 2. Minimum work output 3. Not challenged by school work, poorly motivated	1. Realistic skill assessment 2. Value education, learning 3. Confrontive, persuasive 4. Empowering, enthusiastic	1. Establish purpose 2. Goal achievement 3. Monitor comprehension—paraphrasing, predicting 4. Strategies for all subjects and reflection on their use

REFERENCES

Bandura, A. (1997). *Self-Efficacy: The Exercise of Control*. New York: W.H. Freeman.

Barkley, R. (1990). *Attention Deficit-Hyperactivity Disorder: A Handbook for Diagnosis and Treatment*. New York: Guilford Press.

Black, H., & Black, S. (1990). *Book II—Organizing Thinking: Graphic Organizers*. Pacific Grove, CA: Midwest Publications.

Brophy, J. (1996). *Teaching Problem Students*. New York: Guilford Press.

Cawalti, G. (Ed.) (1995). *Handbook of Research on Improving Student Achievement*. Arlington, VA: Educational Research Service.

Choate, J. S. (1993). *Successful Mainstreaming: Proven Ways to Detect and Correct Special Needs*. Boston: Allyn and Bacon.

Conti-D'Antonio, M., Bertrando, R., & Eisenberger, J. (1998). *Supporting Students with Learning Needs in the Block*, Larchmont, NY: Eye On Education.

Costa, A. L. (1990). *The School as Home for the Mind*. Palatine, IL: Skylight Publishing.

Dawson, P. (1994, June). Homework survival guide. *Communique, 22* (8).

Deschler, D. D., & Schumaker, J. B. (1984). Learning strategies: An instructional alternative for low achieving adolescents. *Exceptional Children, 52,* 583–590.

DuPaul, G., & Stoner, G. (1994). *ADHD in the Schools: Assessment and Intervention Strategies.* New York: Guilford Press.

Ellis, D. B. (1991). *Becoming a Master Student.* Rapid City, SD: College Survival.

Ellis, E. S. (1991). An instrumental model for teaching learning strategies. *Focus on Exceptional Children, 23,* 1–24.

Ellis, E. S. (1997). Watering up the curriculum for adolescents with learning disabilities. *Remedial and Special Education, 18,* 326–346.

Ellis, E. S. (1999). *Using Graphic Organizers to Make Sense of the Curriculum.* Tuscaloosa, AL: Masterminds.

Gaskins, E., & Elliot, T. (1991). *Implementing Cognitive Strategy Training Across the School.* Philadelphia, PA: Brookline Books.

Hallowell, E., & Ratey, J. (1995). *Answers to Distraction.* New York: Pantheon Books.

Hughes, C. (1999, Spring). Helping adolescents with learning disabilities become strategic learners. *Bridges, Research into Practice.* State College, PA: Penn State.

Kounin, G. (1970). Discipline and group management in classrooms. In Brophy, J. (Ed.) (1996), *Teaching Problem Students* (pp. 10–11). New York: Holt, Rinehart & Winston.

Landfried, S. E. (1989). "Enabling" undermines responsibility in students. *Education Leadership, 47,* 61–65.

Levine, M. (1993). *All Kinds of Minds.* Cambridge, MA: EPS.

Meltzer, L. (1992). *Strategy Use in Students with Learning Disabilities: The Challenge of Assessment, Strategy Assessment and Instruction for Students with Learning Disabilities: From Theory to Practice.* Austin, TX: Pro-Ed.

Meltzer, L. (Ed.) (1993). *Strategy Assessment and Instruction for Students with Learning Disabilities—From Theory to Practice.* Austin, TX: Pro-Ed.

Nadeau, K., Dixon, E., & Biggs, S. (1993). *School Strategies for ADD Teens.* Chesapeake, MD: Psychological Publications.

Perrone, V. (1994). How to engage students in learning. *Educational Leadership, 51,* 11–13.

Rimm, S. (1997, April). An underachievement epidemic. *Education Leadership, 54*(7), 19–22.

Tomlinson, C. A. (1999). *The Differentiated Classroom, Responding to the Needs of All Learners*. Alexandria, VA: Association for Supervision and Curriculum Development.

Udvari-Solner, A., & Thousand, J. S. (1995). Promising practices that foster inclusive education. In Villa, R. A., & Thousand, J. S. (Eds.), *Creating an Inclusive School* (pp. 110–124). Alexandria, VA: Association for Supervision and Curriculum Development.

Wiggins, G. (1993). Standards, not standardization. *Educational Leadership, 48,* 18–25.

Wiggins, G., & McTaig, J. (1998). *Understanding by Design.* Alexandria, VA: Association for Supervision and Curriculum Development.

Wong, H., & Wong, R. (1998). *The First Day of School.* Mountainview, CA: Harry K. Wong.

3

LEARNING TO LEARN— EXERCISES THAT PROMOTE EFFICACY

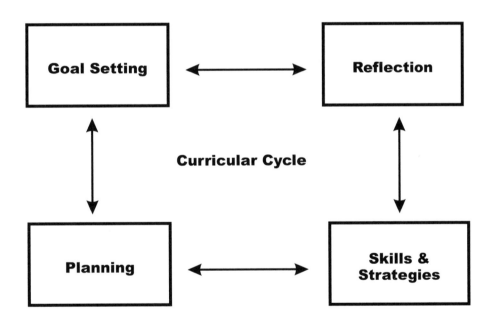

Responsible inclusion requires a continuum of service for students with learning needs. The majority of these students are well served through general education classes with appropriate accommodations and modifications. However, some students require cooperative planning between the special education support teacher and the content teacher to differentiate instruction and build in multiple ways for all students to learn and show what they know, understand, and can do. Other students need classes that are both cooperatively planned and taught so that they can learn. Still other students have learning needs that are unique enough that they must be taught how to face the gaps in their knowledge, skills, and competencies and be given experience with guided practice in the skills necessary to manage school and life outside of school.

Support teachers will still need to teach some students in small groups outside the content classroom to meet their unique needs. However, the primary focus of these groups can no longer be tutorial. If students are to succeed in inclusive schools and enter society as autonomous adults, the support teachers must see their role as teaching for self-efficacy and independence. While working in the content area in which the student is deficient, support teachers and general education teachers must design exercises and tasks that teach students to regulate their motivation and study environment, to control their learning and memory strategies, and to be reflective. These instructional exercises should bolster the students' beliefs in their academic efficacy and build the skills needed for them to fulfill their aspirations. The students should be guided, given feedback, and reinforced positively as they persistently practice the application of skills and strategies in the face of difficulties, stressors, and competing social attractions.

Although many of the following exercises can be performed efficiently in the intimacy of a learning support classroom, most can easily be merged into the routine of a general education course. Each is part of a recursive pattern of goal setting, planning, metacognitive use of strategies, and reflection.

Within the recursive pattern of goal setting, planning, metacognitive use of strategies, and reflection, students will need instruction and guided practice to select and structure their own academic environment. To exercise self-efficacious behaviors, students need to develop the skills to establish a consistent study environment and to mobilize and sustain motivation through goal activation. These include the skill to:

- Establish and achieve proximal goals;
- Maintain regular times and regular places of study;
- Recognize and control the activities that interfere with the completion of academic tasks;
- Practice temporary self-denial when faced with attractive alternatives to study;
- Reflect on and choose to improve academic skills.

Students also need exercises designed to give them instruction and practice in establishing control over their learning and memory. Through this series of exercises, students strengthen their ability to select appropriate study strategies when they need to construct for meaning and manage information. These include the skill to:

- Select strategies for condensing, paraphrasing, and synthesizing information to construct for meaning;
- Identify and record key information from discussion, lecture, and texts;
- Organize information into recallable chunks;
- Rehearse information in preparation of summative tests;
- Reflect on the use of and effectiveness of strategies.

Finally, students need instruction and guided practice in planning for transition from one school level to the next, and, ultimately, to college or work. These skills include the ability to request appropriate accommodations and to make decisions based on factual information as well as the skill to:

- Know and use information about learning styles and multiple intelligence;
- Know, request, and use appropriate accommodations;
- Explore, discuss, and relate current skill levels to the next level of school and life;
- Reflect on and choose to improve metacognitive skills and strategies.

GOAL SETTING

There are various entry points within the recursive pattern of Goal Setting, Planning, metacognitive uses of Strategies, and Reflection. Teachers should decide the best entry points for instruction based on the needs of the student and the demands of the general curriculum. Recognizing where to enter this recursive cycle, and the direction in which to move through the cycle, requires teachers to identify opportunities for instruction. These opportunities become apparent during liaison meetings, cooperative planning meetings, transition planning, and observations of the students. Curriculum artifacts and teacher knowledge of the general curriculum can provide additional data that support instructional decisions. For example, grades on a report card can provide an authentic opportunity for the teacher to guide the student into Goal Setting that sets the stage for practicing self-efficacious behavior and decision making.

Goals become motivators and foster positive attitudes toward academic activities when they are specific, clear, and challenging, but attainable through effort. Learning to set and achieve goals is a skill necessary for students to exert control over their academic environment, but students need instruction in setting such goals. When goals are set unrealistically high, even substantial effort produces failure and undermines personal efficacy. Easy goals arouse very little interest or effort. Simple declarations to "do better" or "work harder" do not result in an increase of efficacy or academic progress, no matter how sincere the promise.

Goals that lead to efficacious behavior (see Figure 3.1) must be measurable, firmly anchored in the student's personal values, be achievable without over-reliance on someone else, and contain a time frame for achievement. It is also best for the goals to be published in some form. An unrecorded goal is only a wish and not as likely to be achieved. Effective goals are set in an hierarchal fashion. Long-term goals are needed to provide purpose and directions, but mid- and short-term goals are needed to focus attention and effort. Because time seems to be available in abundance when goals are too far into the future, a series of subgoals, should be arranged in ascending order. The student response in Figure 3.1 clearly illustrates the power of goal setting.

FIGURE 3.1. A STUDENT EXPLAINS THE POWER OF GOAL SETTING

Facilitators: What helped you improve your performance?

> This class helped me to achieve my goals. I didn't even have goals before I came here. It was helpful because I stayed focused and was given help I needed.

There are abundant opportunities to set goals that are authentic: the beginning of a unit; 3 to 5 days before a summative test; at interim; at the beginning of a marking period; at the beginning of a culminating project or activity. The activities discussed in this chapter teach students to set goals that will motivate and enhance personal efficacy.

The beginning of long-term projects is an excellent time for instruction in goal setting. The purpose of the instruction is to teach students a goal-setting routine that breaks difficult goals into smaller related goals. The primary goal is then expressed as a series of intentions that are spread out over time. The instruction in goal setting can be combined with instruction in planning so that students can receive the guided practice and efficacy training they need to achieve their worthy intentions. The goal-setting example in Figure 3.2 combines goal setting with goal visualization.

FIGURE 3.2. A GOAL-SETTING ACTIVITY FOR A LONG-TERM PROJECT

Science Fair Goal Setting

Directions: *Follow the six steps below to identify your science fair goals and to visualize yourself completing what* **you** *intend to accomplish.*

1. In your science journal, write your goal for the science fair project.

    Be positive about what you intend to do and be willing to take a risk.

    Challenge yourself but be realistic—give yourself the opportunity to succeed.

    Break your largest goal into a series of smaller goals—what is your goal for this week? Next week?

2. Break your goal into a series of intentions—what you intend to do between now and the due date to achieve your goal.

    Avoid writing in the negative—don't tell what you will not do.

    Leave out words like "hope," "try," "harder," or "good."

    Be specific about what you intend to do—what will it look like?

3. Set deadlines for each of your intentions and record each step in your assignment notebook.

4. Consider how you might sabotage your own intentions.

    Have you made your goals dependent on you alone?

    How might you cause your own failure?

    What are the chances of you achieving your goals?

5. Relax, close your eyes, and picture yourself completing what you intended to accomplish.

    Notice how you feel.

6. Write a goal affirmation sentence in your journal.

Special education and general education teachers can teach and reinforce goal setting and the hierarchal nature of efficacious goals by requiring students with learning needs to use their Individualized Educational Plan (IEP) goals as part of their goal-setting routine. These students can then periodically reflect on their goal attainment and become an invaluable contributor to the creation of new goals during the IEP revision process. Figure 3.3 illustrates a student who has used his Annual IEP Goal (to establish and maintain an organizational system for school materials) to set his academic goals.

FIGURE 3.3. A STUDENT USES ANNUAL IEP GOALS TO SET ACADEMIC GOALS

Long-Term
End of this school year
(Set at least one goal)

**1. I want to get higher
grades but not to high,
maby a C+ or B+**

Short-Term
End of third marking period
(Set at least three goals that are concrete,
achievable, measurable, and challenging)

**1. Improve my Math Notebook to an A.
2. Raise my hand when I need to speek.
3. Do my hardest homework first, and easiest last,
so I can be done faster, more efficient thus
putting my grades higher.**

Why are these goals important to you? **I want to get higher grades, higher
my self-esteem; but I don't want grades to high, my parents would
expect more from me.**

What will you do differently to achieve these goals? **Use the straightegie
taught in my support classes.**

Sometimes, goals are more meaningful if they flow naturally from an honest self-appraisal and have a strong connection to the next stage of a student's life as shown in Figure 3.4.

**FIGURE 3.4. A STUDENT SETS GOALS USING
ACADEMIC STRENGTHS AND WEAKNESSES**

Strengths—List at least four things you know and do that lead to school success	Weaknesses—List at least four things you do or habits you have that get in the way of school success
Study for tests	Compleating all homework
listen to teachers	following directions
hand in all outside projects	ask for help
	paying attention during class

Directions: Set three goals for the fourth marking period. Each goal must be specific, clear, and challenging but attainable through your own efforts. Each goal must be something that is important to you and that you are willing to work toward achieving.

1. **Must do all homework in eng. math. geo. s.s.**
2. **Study for all tests in Learning to Learn class**
3. **get no F's or d's on report card**

Why are these goals important to you? **These goals are important to me because I need better grades to pass this year and to go to vo-tech.**

What will you need to do differently to achieve your fourth marking period goals? **I will listen to teachers and make time to study and do home work.**

One of the more important functions of goal setting is the connection students begin to make between their school performance and their life aspirations. An example of one student's reflection on her goal attainment is found in Figure 3.5.

FIGURE 3.5. A STUDENT REFLECTS ON THE PURPOSE OF HER GOAL ATTAINMENT

"Goals"

My goals are important to me because I don't want to end up like my older brother, 20 years old and living at home with a slim chance at a real life. I also want to get out of Unionville and into the real world while being able to handle living independantly.

Exercises in goal setting and achievement can be easily related to any subject. The exercises shown in Figure 3.6 are easily adapted to any activity.

FIGURE 3.6. SEVERAL GOAL-SETTING EXERCISES

Expectations

As we read in _____, people have expectations that influence our behaviors. Often the expectations we have for ourselves come from the expectations that others have for us. These expectations influence our behaviors in positive and negative ways.

Directions:

1. Identify three people in your life who hold expectations for you. Using magazines or personal drawings, find a picture or symbol of each person. Be sure to include yourself on the list.

2. Affix the pictures to a page in your Thinking Journal and write an expectations statement that each would have of you.

3. Develop a response statement that each would have if you improved your self-efficacy skills.

4. Write a paragraph in your journal describing your feelings about meeting the expectations of the people in your life.

Thinking Journal Prompts Directions: *Complete the following statements in your Thinking Journal.*

The Math goal I was most focused on this week was _____.

It was hard for me to _____.

I was surprised to learn _____.

The strategy that helped me the most was _____.

Smoke and Mirrors

1. Self Questioning:

   What are some good things that could happen if I improved my
      Social Studies test scores?

   What are some bad things that could happen if I improved my
      Social Studies test scores?

2. Set Goals:

   Long-Term (End of School Year) _____

   Mid-Term (End of First Semester) _____

   Short-Term (End of First Marking Period) _____

3. Affirmation—I will share my goals with _____

4. Reflection—I will discuss my progress toward my goals on
      _____ (date)

REFLECTION

There are various entry points within the recursive pattern of Reflection,
Goal Setting, Planning, and metacognitive uses of Strategies. Teachers should
decide the best entry points for instruction based on the needs of the student
and the demands of the general curriculum. Deciding to begin with Reflection
requires teachers to identify opportunities for instruction in Reflection. These

opportunities become apparent during liaison meetings, cooperative planning meetings, transition planning, and observations of the students. Curriculum artifacts and teacher knowledge of the general curriculum can provide additional data that support instructional decisions. For example, poor results on an Algebra quiz can prove to be an authentic rationale for the teacher to begin the cycle with Reflection.

Providing time for students to think, talk, and write about their learning, their current level of skill development, their effective use of strategies, and their goal achievement is essential for developing self-efficacy. Learning how to be reflective and to self assess is a necessary precursor and is a fundamental part of personal growth and change. Reflection promotes the union of will and skill and activates a person's willingness to make choices and to accept challenges (Paris, 1994). It allows students to take control of their own progress and learning and to develop the self-efficacy necessary to persist in overcoming obstacles through effort. Through reflection, students can develop:

♦ Self-direction and autonomy

♦ Sense of what they can do and what they can improve

♦ Metacognitive awareness of the strategies they are using

♦ Ability to participate honestly in the evaluation process

Given instruction and the time to reflect on their own performances and accomplishments, students will exercise control over and accept responsibility for the choices they make. Reflective students will develop an internal locus of control, and, because they view their academic progress as their personal obligation, they focus on constructing for meaning and internalizing standards and processes. These students will demonstrate satisfaction with the completion of difficult tasks because they are consciously using their strengths or using bypass strategies to overcome their weaknesses. Reflective students are aware of their levels of motivation, their own skills and talents, and the effort that it takes to persist in the face of difficulties or in the presence of distractions. Reflective students consider and consciously make decisions about their work and study habits. They monitor the effectiveness of the strategies they have chosen and have alternative strategies to choose from if their original choice is not working. Finally, these students are knowledgeable about their successes and failures, plan for future improvement, and map out their intentions. They possess a keen sense of self-efficacy.

Because students can become detached and disengaged if they are not provided frequent opportunities to reflect on their progress and learning, special and general education teachers must model reflective behaviors and provide students with the time to learn and practice the skills involved with reflective thought (see Figure 3.7). Whereas it is important for general education teachers to plan and embed frequent opportunities for reflection in to everyday instruction, it is critical for special education teachers to do so. The school day is filled with opportunities for reflection. Some of these opportunities are:

FIGURE 3.7. A STUDENT REFLECTS ON HIS USE OF STRATEGIES

Am I Where I Want To Be?

Directions: Prepare for a conference with the instructor by thinking about the answers to these questions.

♦ Are you using your strategies regularly?

Yes. There are helping me get my work done.

♦ Are the strategies making a difference in your school success?

Yes. I am getting better grades.

♦ Do you still need to strengthen any of the categories?

Yes. Math. I need a better grade.

♦ Before and after summative evaluations;
♦ Before and after formative assessments;
♦ Before, during, and after projects;
♦ Before, during, and after reading;
♦ Before and after parent conferences;
♦ At the beginning and end of a marking period.

To become reflective thinkers, students need an environment that allows for setbacks and errors. The students must have the vocabulary of reflections and abundant opportunities for validation. Teaching students a simple reflective routine and then using that same routine throughout the school year helps the process of reflective thought become a routine. One such exercise is shown in Figure 3.8.

FIGURE 3.8. A STUDENT REFLECTION ROUTINE

Read your IEP goals and your goal-setting pyramid. Complete a journal entry answering the following questions:

♦ **Progress:** Have you reached your goals? Why or why not?

♦ **Facilitator:** What is helping you or what did you do to get closer to or reach your goal?

♦ **Obstacles:** What is in the way or is slowing you down as you try to reach your goal?

♦ **Growth:** What did you learn in the past weeks that you can use in the next weeks?

♦ **Intentions:** What will you do differently in the future?

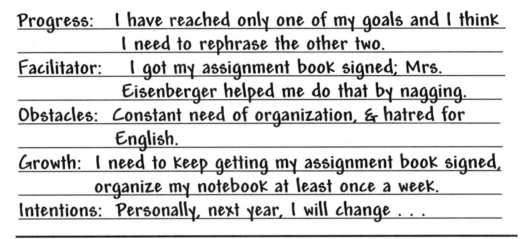

Progress: I have reached only one of my goals and I think I need to rephrase the other two.

Facilitator: I got my assignment book signed; Mrs. Eisenberger helped me do that by nagging.

Obstacles: Constant need of organization, & hatred for English.

Growth: I need to keep getting my assignment book signed, organize my notebook at least once a week.

Intentions: Personally, next year, I will change . . .

A simple and efficient method of reflection is to have students summarize their intentions, formalize those intentions into a list or journal entry, and to periodically reflect on their ability to maintain those intentions. Figure 3.9 is an example of this student-teacher interaction. Teachers can keep students grounded in reality by suggesting reflection in areas the student may not have considered.

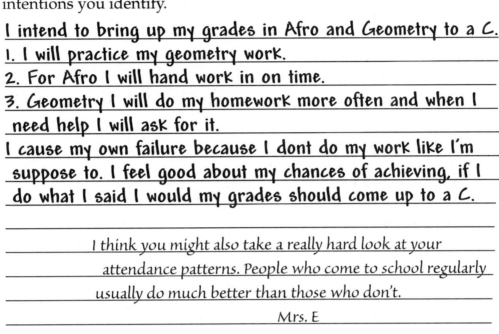

FIGURE 3.9. A STUDENT IDENTIFIES HIS INTENTIONS AND A TEACHER RESPONDS

Directions: List three intentions for third marking period and explain how you feel about your chances of being successful in keeping the intentions you identify.

I intend to bring up my grades in Afro and Geometry to a C.

1. I will practice my geometry work.

2. For Afro I will hand work in on time.

3. Geometry I will do my homework more often and when I need help I will ask for it.

I cause my own failure because I dont do my work like I'm suppose to. I feel good about my chances of achieving, if I do what I said I would my grades should come up to a C.

I think you might also take a really hard look at your attendance patterns. People who come to school regularly usually do much better than those who don't.

Mrs. E

One of the best opportunities for reflection follows a summative evaluation. If students are to exercise control over their academic progress, a method of critiquing tests needs to guide students through an examination of their preparation. Even when a students do well on a test, they can profit from a reflection on their performance. Figure 3.10 is one method of student reflection about test performance.

FIGURE 3.10. A STUDENT CRITIQUES HIS TEST PERFORMANCE

---

1. ANALYSIS (✘)

✔ I should have started to prepare sooner than I did. ⟶

___ I did not schedule enough time for preparation.

___ I did the teacher-assigned home-work and thought my preparation was adequate.

___ I should have prepared a splash-down.

___ I should have picked a different strategy for preparation.

___ I prepared for recognition when I needed recall.

___ I was overconfident.

___ I studied the wrong information

___ I had trouble understanding the questions or instructions.

✔ I had trouble with the format of the test. ⟶

___ I made careless mistakes.

___ I ran out of time.

✔ I guessed too much.

✔ I choked or "blanked out" during the test.

✔ I was unfamiliar with parts of the test.

✔ I remember seeing the material but could not "pull" the information from my memory.

___ I misinterpreted what some of the questions were asking.

___ Other _____

3. POSSIBLE SOLUTIONS (✎)

Begin post-it process as soon as Chapter is assignment.

Do all of the hard assignments in Learning to Learn

Ask for assistance to clarify the test.

Talk out chapter with study partner and identify Key information

2. CONCLUSIONS (✎) **I need to study all critical information**
—I need to ask for clarification.
—I need to start preparing for the tests as soon as we start
   another chapter.

Reflection does not need to be lengthy to be effective and to promote effica-cious behavior. Figure 3.11 shows several short reflections.

FIGURE 3.11. PROMPTS FOR REFLECTION

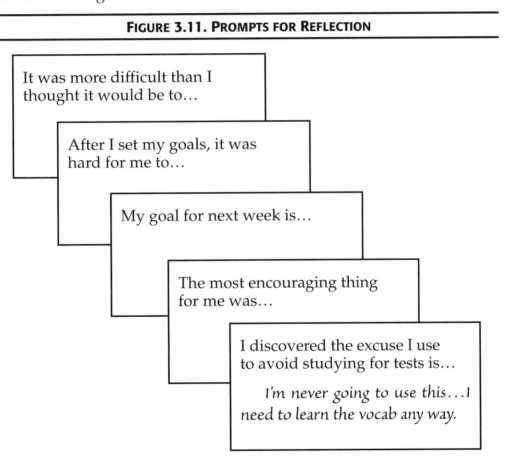

It was more difficult than I
thought it would be to…

After I set my goals, it was
hard for me to…

My goal for next week is…

The most encouraging thing
for me was…

I discovered the excuse I use
to avoid studying for tests is…

*I'm never going to use this…I
need to learn the vocab any way.*

PLANNING

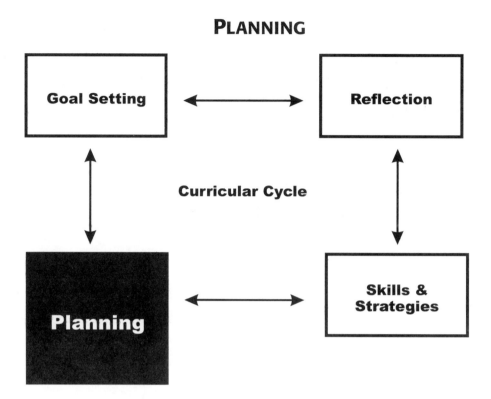

There are various entry points within the recursive pattern of Planning, Goal Setting, metacognitive uses of Strategies, and Reflection. Teachers should decide the best entry points for instruction based on the needs of the student and the demands of the general curriculum. Recognizing where to enter this recursive cycle, and the direction in which to move through the cycle, requires teachers to identify opportunities for instruction. These opportunities become apparent during liaison meetings, cooperative planning meetings, transition planning, and observations of the students. Curriculum artifacts and teacher knowledge of the general curriculum can provide additional data that support instructional decisions. For example, a student's failure to complete and submit homework provides authentic opportunities for the teacher to begin the cycle with Planning.

Planning is the process of combining multiple learning strategies to accomplish academic goals. To plan effectively, students must have a variety of strategies from which to choose and the time to reflect and consider what they would like to achieve. Planning skills include predicting, organizing, and checking. Students who are efficacious planners sequence the actions they will take to meet the demands of a particular task. They select specific strategies that are appropriate for the task or combine several strategies into a workable scheme. They are also able to monitor the effectiveness of their plans and adjust or correct when necessary, dropping and replacing strategies that are not working well. Students who have a strong belief in their efficacy are quicker to discard strategies that are not working, and they consistently and effectively apply what they know (Bandura, 1997).

Because many students with learning needs have difficulty shifting flexibly among different approaches, difficulty coordinating the strategies needed to learn effectively, and difficulty identifying useful planning and checking strategies, specific instructions and guided practice are necessary. In school, authentic opportunities abound to teach students the skills needed to be efficacious planners. One way to teach students planning skills is to have them identify the obstacle they believe is preventing learning and to have them plan a solution. Teachers should help extend the plan into a more complete solution. One student's plan is shown in Figure 3.12.

**FIGURE 3.12. A STUDENT IDENTIFIES AN
OBSTACLE AND PLANS THE SOLUTION**

I want B level grades

Obstacle	Solution
Not on task—Poor listening.	Sit close to the front in all classes or close to the teacher.
	You might also write down what the teachers says. Mrs. E

Students need opportunities to reflect on their planning skills and to identify areas of weakness. Teachers need to teach students to plan just as they would teach any other skill. In Figure 3.13, a student reflects on his skills and identifies an area needing correction.

FIGURE 3.13. A STUDENT MONITORS HIS PLANNING SKILLS

> **4 = Mastered:** I do this automatically. This is part of my school behavior. No one has to remind me.
>
> **3 = Good:** I know how to do this but I sometimes have to be reminded. Even though I know this will help me be more successful, I don't do this automatically.
>
> **2 = Needs Work:** I know I should do this but I often need to be reminded. I only do this when an adult suggests this or reminds me it needs to be done.
>
> **1 = Not Yet:** I only do this when I am forced to or when I am being observed. I refuse to do this or I do not think this is necessary for me.

Comments:

Student **I think I have improved in most areas besides reading directions.**

Skill Area	Student	Teacher
Self-Assigned Homework		
Writing	1	1
Projects	1	1
Practice	3	3
Test Preparation	3	3
Keeping Track		
Homework	4	4
Projects	4	4
Test Preparations	3	3
Materials	4	4
Grades	3	3
Strategy Repertoire		
Names, Steps	3	3
Variety	3	3
Matches Learning Style	3	3
Monitors Effectiveness	3	3

Because many students with learning needs have difficulty organizing multiple strategies into a coherent plan, a framework may need to be given to the student. Figure 3.14 is an Objective Test-Taking Cycle frame.

FIGURE 3.14. A STUDENT PLANS FOR THE MANY STRATEGIES NEEDED TO PREPARE FOR A TEST

Steps	*Possible Strategies*			*Personal Plan*
1. Set Goal: target a grade establish a time frame commit to strategies	Conferencing	Journalizing	Pyramid	conference
2. Identify the key information	Graphic Organizer Clustering Math Attack Color Coding	Cued Notes Highlighting Flash Cards Skimming	3-Fold Page Cornell Notes Post-Its Muscle Reading	post it's
3. Memorize the information	Walk About Do & Redo Acronyms Oral Rehearsal	Study Partner Peer Teacher Splashdown 3-Fold Page	Overlearning Write/Read Key Word Pic.	keyword pic.
4. Check memory	Practice Test Oral Retrieval Walk About	Study Partner 3-Fold Page Flash Cards	Cover & Recite Splashdown Computer Drill	practice test
5. Adjust target grade	Reward Yourself	Goal Setting	Accepting Feedback	Accepting feedback
6. Repeat Steps 3–5	I will repeat: 1 2 3 4 5			2 times
7. Take Test	Visualizations Eliminate Options Peek-a-boo Using Margins	Splashdown Steal It Triage Easy to Hard	Oral Retrieval Cued Notes SCORER Fore/Back	peek-a-boo steal it—talk it
8. Critique Test Performance	Reward Yourself Skill Evaluation	Conclusions Requesting Help	5 Whys Consequences	Critique
9. Adjust Strategies	Responding to Persuasion Decision Making	Responding to Help Requesting Help		
Repeat the cycle				

Students need time to reflect on planning, but the reflection need not be extremely time-consuming. Figure 3.15 shows several quick but thought-provoking prompts for thinking about planning.

**FIGURE 3.15. SEVERAL QUICK PROMPTS
FOR REFLECTING ON PLANNING SKILL**

STRATEGIES

There are various entry points within the recursive pattern of metacognitive uses of Strategies, Goal Setting, Planning, and Reflection. Teachers should decide the best entry points for instruction based on the needs of the student and the demands of the general curriculum. Recognizing where to enter this recursive cycle, and the direction in which to move through the cycle, requires teachers to identify opportunities for instruction. These opportunities become apparent during liaison meetings, cooperative planning meetings, transition planning, and observations of the students. Curriculum artifacts and teacher knowledge of the general curriculum can provide additional data that support instructional decisions. For example, when a student asks a question of his or her support teacher that is better answered by the general education teacher, an authentic opportunity for instruction of a self-advocacy strategy is presented.

Learning strategies are tactics and self-management processes that individuals use while learning. The use of strategies requires effortful processing and is difficult for students unless efficacy skills are in place. Students with learning needs are generally weaker in the number of learning strategies that they know and use spontaneously than their same-age peers who do not have learning needs (Meltzer, 1993). Students with learning needs are less able to select strategies that match academic tasks. These students do not readily make connections between their efficacious use of the strategies and their success in a task (see Figure 3.16), often attributing success to external forces such as an "easy" test. It is critical for general education and special education teachers to teach the student to make the connection between the application of a particular strategy and success in an academic task.

**FIGURE 3.16. A STUDENT DESCRIBES THE DIFFICULTY INVOLVED
WITH THE ACQUISITION OF A NEW STRATEGY**

Getting my assinmnet notebook signed is important to me
because Mrs. Eis. said it would help me stay organized, also,
part of my Learning to Learn grade relys on it. I will know I
achieved it if Mrs. Eis. stops telling me to get it signed and . . .
. . . congradulates me for getting it done. It is
challenging because I am very lazy.

Students with learning needs are also less able to learn strategies effortlessly. They are clumsy in their execution and application, especially if the strategy is new. Because the initial use of strategies requires an increase in work time, these students will abandon strategies too soon and persist in using less effective strategies. The efficacious use of strategies requires a substantial amount of time and effort, and both the special education teacher and the general education teacher must provide guided practice and a substantial amount of feedback during the cycle of learning described in Figure 3.17

FIGURE 3.17. LEARNING A NEW STRATEGY

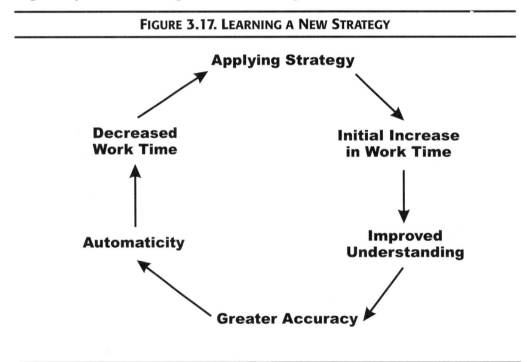

Learning strategies are maintained and transferred to new situations if the students understand their value and can connect the strategy to an improvement in performance (Meltzer, 1992). To produce efficacious students, teachers in special education classes must focus on how to select, use, and monitor strategies, and teachers in general education classes must design lessons that incorporate strategy training and use. The student's reflections can guide needed instruction, as the student's journal entry in Figure 3.18 demonstrates.

**FIGURE 3.18. A STUDENT IDENTIFIES A STRATEGY
DEFICIENCY AND THE TEACHER RESPONDS**

. . . need to put in effort. I have trouble guessing what will be on a test and when I get nervous I can't think at all. I still need to learn to calm down because I do go into exams prepared.

Good insight. We will pick a "calming" strategy for next marking period.

Mrs. E.

To be most successful when selecting and using strategies, students must be aware of their learning preferences and intelligence strengths. The journal entry in Figure 3.19 demonstrates how choosing strategies based on learning style can benefit students.

**FIGURE 3.19. A STUDENT EXPLAINS THE PROCESS OF
ADOPTING STRATEGIES BASED ON LEARNING STYLE**

I learns better when the material is read out ~~load~~ loud by someone else or myself. My strategies match my learning style. I have a reader for tests when I don't understand a question. I also review for my test outloud before taking it. This gives me clear studying. I also like ~~the~~ to write down my strategy when I used my daily lessons plan. This way I can figure out what I'm doing and how I'm doing it correctly

---

Being aware of how strategies function is another key component in the successful adoption of the processes and skills needed for self-efficacy. One way to ensure that students transfer their strategies with them to other content classes is to have them regularly explain which strategies they find useful. Figure 3.20 is an example of this technique.

**FIGURE 3.20. A STUDENT REVIEWS HIS
STRATEGIES AND EXPLAINS THEIR PURPOSE**

Strategy	*Directions: Circle the strategies you are using and explain how you use each.*
SELF-DETERMINATION: 　Goal Setting/Achievement 　Accepting Feedback 　5 Whys 　Requesting Help 　Behavior Checklist 　Responding to Persuasion 　Self-progress Report 　Unhelpful Thoughts 　Positive Self-Talk	I request help with assignments. I use this to do assignments.
MEMORIZING: 　Key Word Pictures 　Highlighting 　Oral Rehearsal/Retrieval 　Chunking 　Flash Cards 　Study Partner 　Cover and Recite 　Do and Redo	Use sounds to help me memorize Use it because I get better grades I use this because it helps me remember
TEST TAKING: 　Test Preparation Routine 　Test Critique 　Steal It 　Splashdown 　Eliminating Options 　Test Vocalization 　Math Checklist	I take stuff off other parts of tests. Helps get better grades
ORGANIZING: 　Assignment & Grade Tracking 　Long-term Assignment Planning 　Prioritizing 　Notebook & Locker Organization 　Hard to Easy 　Easy First 　Materials Management Checklist 　Post-It Process 　Chunking	It helps me to get assignments in on time Makes work seem faster I use this on tests and homework

COMPOSING: Graphic Organizers Steal It Oral Rehearsals Stop and Think Editing Partner Power Writing	I use these to organize and web Steal it helps my spelling on test
UNDERSTANDING: Post-It Process Stop and Think Cornell/3-Column Note Taking Math Attack Muscle and Reciprocal Reading	In Math Homework I use this.

When students' strategies become automatic, a shift in thinking occurs. The students begin to discuss their use of strategies as part of their abilities. This shift is clearly demonstrated in Figure 3.21.

FIGURE 3.21. A STUDENT DESCRIBES HER SUCCESS AFTER A YEAR OF INTENSIVE STRATEGY INSTRUCTION

What have you learned this year that you will be able to use next year?

I have learned that I actually can do good in school. I think last year I underestimated my abilities and now I am using my abilities to my advantage.

Is your bank of strategies full enough to meet next year's academic demands?

For now, my strategy bank is full enough but I hope when I hit a problem I will find a new strategy to add to help me out.

To become comfortable with strategies and to make them part of their efficacious patterns, students need to be aware of how they use strategies to learn, organize, and control the environment in which they work, and to transfer those strategies into other areas of their lives. Simple, quick reflections, as shown in Figure 3.22, reveal how well the students are acquiring strategies.

FIGURE 3.22. STUDENTS EXPLAIN HOW STRATEGIES ENABLE THEM TO EXERCISE CONTROL AND LEARN

Three strategies that I used today are...

☞ _____
_____

☞ _____
_____

☞ _____
_____

This week, I wished I had a better strategy for...

I was surprised to learn that...
there are strategies to help me learn things. I learned rules for grammer.

Strategies that work

Chairs and Place
I sit by my self so I can consanetrate

Task
Math class doing math problems— less socializing

Other Uses
Science—my best friend is in that class and I tend to goof more with her.

REFERENCES

Bandura, A. (1997). *Self-Efficacy: The Exercise of Control.* New York: W.H. Freeman.

Beyer, B. K. (1991). *Teaching Thinking Skills: A Handbook for Secondary Teachers.* Fairfax, VA: Allyn and Bacon.

Black, H., & Black, S. (1990). *Book II—Organizing Thinking: Graphic Organizers.* Pacific Grove, CA: Midwest Publications.

Bloom, B. S. (1976). *Human Characteristics and School Learning.* New York: McGraw Hill.

Brooks, J. G., & Brooks, M. G. (1995). *In Search of Understanding: The Case for Constructivist Classrooms.* Alexandria, VA: Association for Supervision and Curriculum Development.

Canady, R.L., & Retig, M. D. (1996). *Teaching in the Block: Strategies for Engaging Active Learners.* Larchmont, NY: Eye On Education.

Choate, J. S. (1997). *Successful Inclusion: Proven Ways to Detect and Correct Special Needs.* Boston: Allyn and Bacon.

Conti-D'Antonio, M., Bertrando, R., & Eisenberger, J. (1998). *Supporting Students with Learning Needs in the Block.* Larchmont, NY: Eye on Education.

Costa, A. L. (1985). *Developing Minds: A Resource Book for Teaching Thinking.* Alexandria, VA: Association for Supervision and Curriculum Development.

Costa, A. L. (1990). *The School as Home for the Mind.* Palatine, IL: Skylight Publishing.

Deschler, D. D., & Schumaker, J. B. (1984). Learning strategies: An instructional alternative for low-achieving adolescents. *Exceptional Children, 52,* 583–590.

Ellis, E. S. (1991). An instrumental model for teaching learning strategies. *Focus on Exceptional Children, 23,* 1–24.

Frank, A. R. (1973). Breaking down the learning tasks: A sequence approach. *Teaching Exceptional Children, 6,* 16–19.

Garavaglia, P. (1993). How to ensure the transfer of training. *Training and Development, 47,* 66.

Gaskins, E., & Elliot, T. (1991). *Implementing Cognitive Strategy Training Across the School.* Philadelphia, PA: Brookline Books.

Geocaris, C. (1996). Increasing student engagement, A mystery solved. *Education Leadership, 54,* 72–75.

Goldstein, A. P., Sparfkin, R. P., Geoshaw, J. N., Klein, P. (1980). *Skill Streaming the Adolescent: A Structured Approach to Teaching Prosocial Skills.* Champaign, IL: Research Press Company.

Hughes, C. (1999). Helping adolescents with learning disabilities become strategic learners. *Bridges–Research into Practice*. University Park, PA: Penn State.

McCarney, S. B., Tucci, J. K. (1990). *Study Skills for Students in Our Schools*. Columbia, MO: Hawthorn Press.

Meltzer, L. (1992). *Strategy Use in Students with Learning Disabilities: The Challenge of Assessment, Strategy Assessment and Instruction for Students with Learning Disabilities: From Theory to Practice*. Austin, TX: Pro-Ed.

Meltzer, L. J. (Ed.). (1993). *Strategy Assessment and Instruction for Students with Learning Disabilities—From Theory to Practice*. Austin, TX: Pro-Ed.

Miles, D. D., & Forcht, J. P. (1995). Mathematical strategies for secondary students with learning disabilities or mathematics deficiencies: A cognitive approach. *Intervention in School and Clinic, 31*, 91–96.

Paris, S., & Ayers, L. R. (1994). *Becoming Reflective Students and Teachers with Portfolios and Authentic Assessment*. Washington, DC: American Psychological Association.

Polloway, E. (1996). Treatment acceptability: Determining appropriate intervention within inclusive classrooms. *Intervention in School and Clinic, 31*, 133–144.

Roy, P. A. (1990). *Students Learning Together*. Richfield, MN: Patricia Roy.

4

ASSESSING STUDENT GROWTH IN THE GENERAL CURRICULUM

The 1997 reauthorization of Individuals with Disabilities Education Act (IDEA) requires both general and special education teachers to assess the progress that special education students make in the general curriculum. This significantly changes both the role of teachers and the purpose of assessment. Assessment can no longer be seen as only a summation of what content the student has learned; rather, assessment must provide baseline information about what the student has learned (formative data) that teachers use to guide subsequent lessons.

Previously used exclusively for reporting out, assessments now need to include what students know, understand, and are able to do. They must be broadened to include checking on the degree to which students use a skill and learning whether students are applying the knowledge and skills they have been taught. Assessment, still important for summing up all the skills and concepts students have learned over a particular period of time, must now be an ongoing process of gathering evidence about learning and growth. Assessment, in this expanded format, provides teachers and parents with information about what students currently know, understand, and are able to do in the context of a particular area of study that they, in turn, share with students.

IDEA compels educators to focus on two current initiatives. The first initiative is the need to optimize learning for all students by providing standards-driven differentiated instruction. The second initiative compels educators to make available accurate, useful data about learning. The data must be communicated to students, their teachers, and their parents so that reflection can occur and efficacious student behavior can lead to independence.

Although IDEA has its flaws and opposition to elements of IDEA can be heard in courtrooms, school board chambers, teachers' lunchrooms, and taxpayer group meetings, there is one undeniable fact: special education is everyone's job. Students with learning needs of all types and degrees are currently being educated in general education classrooms, and inclusion is and will continue to be an integral part of public education.

Although the term inclusion is not contained in the law, LRE is. The law states that:

> to the fullest extent appropriate, handicapped children, including those children in public and private institutions or other care facilities, are [to be] educated with children who are not handicapped, and that special classes, separate schooling, or other removal of handicapped children from the regular educational environment [is to] occur only when the nature or severity of the handicap is such that the education in regular classes with the use of supplementary aids and services cannot be achieved satisfactorily (P.L. 94-142, Section 1412 [5] [B]).

IDEA requires that all students be educated within the general curriculum to the fullest extent appropriate and expands the definition of general education curriculum as a continuum of outcomes and skills for people ages 3 to 21 years. Curriculum is defined by IDEA as content, not setting, and declares that content involves all of the activities, materials, instructional techniques, and objectives typically experienced by all the students in the school. Under the federal law, general education curriculum concerns itself with processes as well as content outcomes. This legal mandate forces educators to ensure access for all students to an appropriate education. IDEA has forced educators to examine their practice as well as to test the limits of how inclusion impacts teachers, administrators, and students on a daily basis. IDEA will not go away, and waiting, as educators sometimes do, "for this to pass" will not serve the professional community well. While the requirements of IDEA are tested in the courts, school districts must comply with state regulations in their interpretation of the federal law.

Curriculum-based assessments (CBA) are teacher-designed criterion-referenced tools used to gauge progress in curriculum. They can be used with different types of curricula—developmental, spiraling, or unestablished curricula. CBAs can be developed and can be used with all curricula to assess progress toward general curriculum content standards. Developmental curricula, organized in a hierarchical fashion, builds on the acquisition of prerequisite skills taught at earlier levels. Reading curricula and traditional Algebra are examples of developmental curricula. Spiraling curricula are also organized by level, but the concepts are repeated at subsequent levels. English curricula, for example, repeat the concepts of theme, genre, and conflict, many, many times from the early grades with emergent readers to high school and beyond with more sophisticated learners. Unestablished curricula are those that have been developed by teachers in response to students' needs. The Individualized Education Plan (IEP), with its goals and objectives for student learning, is an example of unestablished curricula.

Curricula make explicit demands on the learner. Curricula are neither neutral nor static, but provide the content standards by which student learning is measured and school programs are compared. Curricula content, methods for instruction, activities, assessments, as well as materials used in the delivery of the curricula, can become obstacles and deterrents to some students with learning needs. For example, if teaching of solving binomials is confined to a two-week period and the teacher lectures and provides only computer scored exams, students who require more time for guided practice and need more frequent feedback on which to reflect and plan may be at a disadvantage. Because curricula are normative learning devices, that is they articulate what students should know, learn, and be able to do on average at a particular grade level, they place explicit demands on the learner to fit within an expected band of performance. Students will distinguish themselves, for example, if they learn at a different rate than other students in the class. The student who needed more time to learn binomials will stand out as deficient in a class of learners who are able to keep pace with the teacher's delivery of the Algebra curriculum.

A comparison between curricula and standardized tests may clarify the normative properties of developmental curricula.

Both curricula and standardized tests:

- Are based on mean or average performance.

- Are used to determine how a student compares to or deviates from the average student.

- Are based on ascending order of skills commensurate with age ranges.

- Are written in reference to grade levels and categorize the greatest number of students at that grade level.

- Require that a certain volume of material be addressed.

- Measure material learned at a specific rate for all.

- Make assumptions that adequate coverage of material has occurred at all levels.

- Are inflexible and assume that students will adapt to it.

- Are designed to address specific materials at given grade levels therefore identify the students who fall outside the range of average.

- Are often sorting devices between those who can and can't.

Curricula has a certain degree of tolerance. The tolerance, a narrow band of what is perceived as normal or average learning by a teacher, varies and depends on teacher training, teacher ability to differentiate instruction, and teacher willingness to adapt to the learning needs of the student. Recently, even the mainstream press has responded to IDEA and the requirement for inclusion and "supplementary aids and services." Jon Leo's "Let's Lower the Bar" (1998), an article written for *US News and World Report,* cites an example of a law student who exercised her right to accommodation. The disabled student took the New York Bar examination on six occasions and used "double time" as an accommodation. Lee questioned whether this mandate to accommodate handicaps in schools and the workplace will lower the standards all of us have come to expect. Lowering standards serves no one and is not the purpose of developing curriculum accommodations for students. Accommodations level the playing field and allow a student to interact with the curriculum at the highest levels possible for that student. The rationale for writing accommodations to a curriculum is to allow students to have a greater likelihood of achieving success by providing bridges to rigorous content standards.

Unfortunately, many people enter the debate over the fair use of accommodations without being completely aware of what accommodations are intended to be. When accommodations are appropriately designed and effectively used, they "level the playing fields" for students who have disabilities but do not change or excuse students from meeting curriculum-content standards. Accommodations fulfill one or more of these functions:

- Assist the student to compensate for the intellectual, physical, sensory or behavioral challenges

- ◆ Allow the student to use current skills while promoting the acquisition of new ones
- ◆ Prevent a mismatch between the student's skills and the general education lesson content
- ◆ Reduce the level of abstraction to make content relevant to the student's current and future life

Accommodations are changes in standard operating procedures without which a student would be unable to obtain a free and appropriate education (FAPE). They are hierarchical and follow naturally from the student's disability or handicap. The accommodations should be in place for instruction, but are often critical during assessment because without the accommodations, it is most likely that assessments will reflect the disability instead of what the student knows, understands, and is able to do.

The list of accommodations that follows (Figures 4.1 through 4.7) are those that are most often identified in accommodation plans and IEPs. There are seven categories: Setting; Presentation; Response; Instructional; Scheduling; Assistive Devices; and Motivational (Thurlow, 1998). These accommodations are the most helpful in "facilitating success for students with disabilities" (Salend, 1995). Some students may require only one of these accommodations; others may need to use two or three accommodations in combination to show best what they know, understand, and can do. Because these accommodations follow the student, they need not be administered in a special setting unless a specific setting is identified in the IEP or 504 Service Agreement and general education and special education teachers may administer them. Teachers should be aware of each student's accommodations through regular liaison meetings with special education teachers. By listening to students as they advocate for their own learning needs and by participating in the IEP process, teachers can more fully understand the need for particular accommodations.

(Text continues on page 91.)

FIGURE 4.1. SETTING ACCOMMODATIONS

During Instruction	Setting Accommodations	During Assessment
Separate Location		
Teacher will: Confirm that student is working successfully in requested location. **Student will:** Complete test request for Small Group or specific test setting Follow test-prep routine	Most requested locations: —small group —quiet place Most useful for: —sustaining attention —editing distractors	**Teacher will:** Send the test to the location requested **Student will:** Report to location requested Answer the test questions
Seating Adaptations		
Teacher will: Provide adapted seating during quiet, guided practice **Student will:** Complete test request for specific test setting or environment Follow test-prep routine	Most requested adaptations: —face the wall —study carrel Most useful for: —sustaining attention —editing distractors	**Teacher will:** Arrange the setting or environment requested **Student will:** Sit where requested Answer the test questions

FIGURE 4.2. PRESENTATION ACCOMMODATIONS

During Instruction	Presentation Accommodations	During Assessment
Read the Test Aloud to the Student		
Teacher will: Read directions, instruction aloud **Student will:** Complete test request for reader Follow test-prep routine	Most often needed for: —vocabulary, reading above level —tests with embedded information	Most useful for students with: —specific reading disabilities —efficiency disabilities —low cognitive ability —poor working memory —visual impairment	**Teacher will:** Read the test aloud word for word Prerecord the test Present test in sign language **Student will:** Listen, answer test questions
Allow Student to Read Test Aloud		
Teacher will: Listen, correct as student reads aloud **Student will:** Read directions, instructions Complete test request for listener Follow test-prep routine	Most often needed when: —developing habit of listening to self —tests have long stems, double negatives, multistep directions —learning to subvocalize	Most useful for: —auditory learners —poor working memory —students who have difficulty editing distractors	**Teacher will:** Listen as student reads Correct reading errors **Student will:** Read aloud Correct errors pointed out by teacher Answer test questions

During Instruction	Presentation Accommodations	During Assessment
	Clarify Instruction, Questions	
Teacher will: Paraphrase at student's request Provide guided practice in highlighting key information **Student will:** Request teacher to paraphrase Complete test request for paraphrasing Follow test-prep routine	Most often needed for: —vocabulary out of level —double negative, "all except" or "all of the above" questions —long stems questions —multistep directions in paragraph form Most useful for: —students who have attention/concentration problems —students with processing disabilities —students with efficiency disabilities —students with low cognitive ability	**Teacher will:** Paraphrase/simplify/reword leaving content vocabulary being tested intact Insert visual prompts (arrows, stop signs) Highlight key words in stem or direction **Student will:** Listen and restate Follow the directions provided by prompts Attend to highlighted words

(Figure continues on next page.)

During Instruction	Presentation Accommodations	During Assessment
	Increased White Space	
Teacher will: Provide template or mask Prompt student to use mask Provide adapted text —enlarged or darkened —fewer items on a page —increased space between items **Student will:** Use template or mask Complete test request for white space Follow test-prep routine	Most often needed when: —information is densely packed on page —font is below 12 points Most useful for: —students who have attention or concentration problems —students who tire easily —students who are visually impaired	**Teacher will:** Provide an enlarged or darker photocopy Provide a template or mask Adapt test—increase space between items Adapt test— limit number of items on page **Student will:** Use the template to increase white space Complete the test

See Figure 4.6, Assistive Devices, page 84, for additional presentation accommodations.

FIGURE 4.3. RESPONSE ACCOMMODATIONS

During Instruction	Response Accommodations	During Assessment
Student-Generated Notes		
Teacher will: Check student-generated notes for accuracy, suggest improvements **Student will:** Prepare set of cued notes, referenced notes, or graphic organizers Complete test request to use notes	Most frequently used for-mats: —graphic organizer —referenced notes —cued notes —word banks Most useful for: —low cognitive ability —inadequate memory, retention —inability to integrate information —extremely poor working memory	**Teacher will:** Distribute the test Monitor to make sure that only materials prepared by the student is used **Student will:** Bring the prepared material to the test Match material on test to notes
Scribe Answers		
Teacher will: Record student responses **Student will:** Use a scribe during instruction Complete test request for a scribe Follow test-prep routine	Most common procedures: —teacher types responses on computer word for word —teacher records responses in longhand word for word Most often used for: —poor working memory —Dysgraphia —physical limitations	**Teacher will:** Record student responses (word for word) **Student will:** Read and answer aloud

(*Figure continues on next page.*)

During Instruction	Response Accommodations	During Assessment
	Answer Directly on the Test	
Teacher will: Prompt student use of eliminating options and splashdowns **Student will:** Use eliminating options, splashdowns Complete test request for answers last Follow test-prep routine	Most often needed when: —learning test-taking skills —eliminating option, splashdowns —discouraging pattern seekers	Most useful for: —sustaining attention to detail —poor working memory —inability to cross midline	**Teacher will:** Distribute the test, re-mind the student to write directly on the test After test is completed, read letters as student fills in scantron or fill in answer sheets stu-dent reads **Student will:** Cross out, splashdown directly on test Record responses di-rectly on test Transfer answers with assistance after test is done
	See Figure 4.6, Assistive Devices, page 84, for additional response accommodations.	

FIGURE 4.4. INSTRUCTIONAL ACCOMMODATIONS

During Instruction	Instructional Accommodations	During Assessment
	Test-Taking Strategies	
Teacher will: Provide test-taking instruction	Most often taught strategies: —Splashdown —Eliminating Options —Steal It —Response Generation —Triage —Check & Recheck —Relax with Black	Most useful for: —students learning test-taking strategies —students with inadequate retention/memory —students who respond to tests with high emotionality
Student will: Request test-taking instruction Follow test-prep routine: —prepare a splashdown —practice test strategies Complete test request for instruction during test		**Teacher will:** Give direct instruction, direction in test-taking strategies during the test Provide cues for use of test-taking strategies such as: —Remember to locate key word —Have you eliminated some of the options? —Was this mentioned anywhere else on the test? **Student will:** Follow the teacher's directions in how to use test-taking strategies Respond to prompts to use test-taking strategies

FIGURE 4.5. SCHEDULING ACCOMMODATIONS

During Instruction	Scheduling Accommodations	During Assessment
	Extended Time	
Teacher will: Instruct students in how to break assignments into smaller subtasks **Student will:** Complete test request for extra time Follow test-prep routine	Extended time* means: —more than 1 period but within a reasonable time frame *Extended time should never be used to replace preparation*	Most useful for: —slow-processing students —auditory learners —teaching test-taking skills —students with poor attention/concentration —students requesting listeners or readers
		Teacher will: Photocopy double-sided tests Divide test into pieces Administer test in small sections **Student will:** Ask teacher to section tests Complete assessment in sections Arrange to complete unfinished sections during next available study or class period
	Frequent Tests	
Teacher will: Prepare small frequent assessments **Student will:** Complete test request for short tests Follow test-prep routine	Most common procedures: —weekly 10-question tests —combine several quiz scores to equal one test	Most useful for: —low cognitive ability —inadequate memory, retention —inability to integrate information —extremely poor working memory
		Teacher will: Administer frequent small tests **Student will:** Complete assessments

Scheduling Accommodations

During Instruction	Scheduling Accommodations	During Assessment
Periodic Breaks		
Teacher will: Observe, report length of student's productive work period **Student will:** Set up a schedule for completing test based on optimal productive work period	Most common procedure: —administer test over several sessions Most useful for: —poor concentration and attention —short attention spans —students who tire easily	**Teacher will:** Split assessment into small separate sections; Administer test over planned days or periods **Student will:** Arrive at location on time; Complete assessment in planned periods
Specific Time		
Teacher will: Confer with student to arrange for assessment to be completed at a specific time **Student will:** Conference with teacher; Plan for specific time to complete assessment	Most common procedures: —administer test at specific time —avoid administering test at specific time Most often used for: —students whose medication dissipates at a specific time —students who have optimal learning or mental processing times	**Teacher will:** Arrange student schedule to match assessment scheduling needs; Administer assessments at specific times **Student will:** Arrive at agreed time for assessment; Complete assessment

FIGURE 4.6. ASSISTIVE DEVICES

During Instruction	*Assistive Device Accommodations*	*During Assessment*
Devices for Mentally Challenged		
Teacher will: Prompt the student to use assistive device during instruction **Student will:** Notify content teacher of the assistive device needed Follow test-prep routine	Most frequently used: —calculator —word processor —Franklin speller —manipulative Most useful for: —low cognitive ability —inadequate memory —extremely poor working memory —a specific learning disability (e.g., spelling, computation)	**Teacher will:** Distribute the test Monitor to ensure the device used is appropriately based on the purpose of the assessment or skill being measured **Student will:** Use the appropriate device
Devices for Physically Challenged		
Teacher will: Prompt the student to use assistive device during instruction **Student will:** Notify content teacher of the assistive device needed Follow test-prep routine	Most frequently used: —pencil grip —page turner —computer —adaptive furniture —text talker converter —speech synthesizer Most useful for: —students with physical disabilities	**Teacher will:** Distribute the test Monitor to ensure the device used is appropriately based on the purpose of the assessment or skill being measured **Student will:** Use the appropriate device

During Instruction	Assistive Device Accommodations	During Assessment
Devices for Hearing Challenged		
Teacher will: Prompt the student to use assistive device during instruction **Student will:** Notify content teacher of the assistive device needed Follow test-prep routine	Most frequently used: —amplification device Most useful for: —students with auditory disabilities	**Teacher will:** Distribute the test Monitor to ensure the device used is appropriately based on the purpose of the assessment or skill being measured **Student will:** Use the appropriate device
Devices for Visually Challenged		
Teacher will: Prompt the student to use assistive device during instruction **Student will:** Notify content teacher of the assistive device needed Follow test-prep routine	Most frequently used: —brailler —tape recorder —magnification devices Most useful for: —students with visual disabilities	**Teacher will:** Distribute the test Monitor to ensure the device used is appropriately based on the purpose of the assessment or skill being measured **Student will:** Use the appropriate device

(Figure continues on next page.)

During Instruction	*Assistive Device Accommodations*	During Assessment
	Devices for Attention Deficit	
Teacher will: Prompt the student to use assistive device during instruction **Student will:** Notify content teacher of the assistive device needed Follow test-prep routine	Most frequently used: —noise buffers —carrels	**Teacher will:** Distribute the test Monitor to ensure the device used is appropriately based on the purpose of the assessment or skill being measured **Student will:** Use the appropriate device
	Most useful for: —students with Attention Deficit Disorder —students with auditory-processing deficits	

Additional assistive devices might be specified for a particular physical, visual, hearing, or mentally challenged student.

FIGURE 4.7. MOTIVATIONAL ACCOMMODATIONS

During Instruction	*Motivational Accommodation*	*During Assessment*
	On-Task Reminders	
Teacher will: Prompt student with on-task reminders	Most often used to: —give positive reinforcement —refocus attention and concentration	**Teacher will:** Monitor student and make comments: "You don't know this answer. Let's guess and go on to the next question or section." "May I help you get started again?"
Student will: Request on-task reminders Follow test-prep routine	Most useful for: —students with efficiency disabilities —students who are slow to begin —perfectionists	**Student will:** Comply with teacher direction Refocus attention Complete test

(Figure continues on next page.)

During Instruction	Motivational Accommodation	During Assessment
	Verbal Prompts to Cue Recall	
Teacher will: Provide verbal prompts to aid recall **Student will:** Request verbal prompts to cue recall during assessments Follow test-prep routine	Most often used for: —completeness of answers Most useful for: —impulsive students —students with impaired retrieval skills	**Teacher will:** Monitor student and make comments: "I know you left information in your head when you answered #4. Tell me more." "You skipped part 2. Please go back to your seat and finish the test." "You and Jon were doing these together yesterday." **Student will:** Comply with teacher prompts Complete test

During Instruction	Motivational Accommodation	During Assessment
	Prompts to Sustain Effort	
Teacher will: Provide prompts to sustain effort	Most often used to: —sustain effort	**Teacher will:** Monitor student and make comments: "You're doing well. I can tell you prepared." "You guessed right. You must have a guardian angel today." "I'm really proud of how well you have begun."
Student will: Request feedback to sustain effort during assessments Follow test-prep routine	Most useful for: —failure syndrome students (quitters) —underachievers —students with low attentional reserves	**Student will:** Sustain effort Complete test

(Figure continues on next page.)

During Instruction	Motivational Accommodation	During Assessment
	Prompts to Complete Assigned Tasks	
	Most often used for:	Most useful for:	
	—home/school communication	—failure syndrome students	
	—recording assignments accurately	—underachievers	
	—maintaining progress on projects	—avoidance behavior	
Teacher will: Periodically check assignment book for accuracy		**Teacher will:** Grade assignment notebook for accuracy and completeness
Periodically check progress on long-term projects		Evaluate student plan for the completion of long-term assignment
Student will: Request teacher check		Assess for the completion of each step
		Student will: Comply with teacher requests

Modifications and changes in district curriculum are designed by a Multi-disciplinary Team (MDT) through the IEP process for students whose disabilities are so severe that they would be unable to demonstrate growth using the district curricula. The MDT identifies what district curriculum is appropriate and orders modified objectives to replace the district objectives during the writing of the IEP. These modifications are required so that even severely disabled students may be educated to the maximum extent possible with their similarly aged peers. The modified standards must be in place for both instruction and assessment for students to be able to demonstrate progress toward their IEP goals.

Although the vast majority of students only require accommodations for assessment and some instructional modifications, a few students may require modifications that make instruction truly different from that of their classmates. These alternative standards are often called functional goals and prepare students for self-care, life skills, and school-to-work opportunities. No teacher should ever modify curriculum without following the IEP process. To do so would constitute the implementation of an IEP or an Accommodation Plan without protecting the due process rights of the student. A parent could correctly construe from this action that their child is in need of the specially designed instruction of an IEP but that the district failed to follow the appropriate legal procedure (Faust, 1998).

One way to design modifications is to use the modification ladder in Figure 4.8.

Critics of special education may be correct when they blame special educators for lowering standards of instruction. It should be a rare occurrence when curriculum goals and objectives are modified for students. Only when MDTs decide that students are unable to learn the critical skills and concepts of content standards should modifications be made. Unfortunately, team members may be more concerned with making school more pleasant and easy for the student than in maintaining appropriately rigorous content supported by the Specially Designed Instruction of the IEP. Using the Curriculum Modification Ladder can help decision makers use concrete criteria when deciding to modify curriculum. Using defensible criteria for modifying curricula can help educators avoid minimizing a student's program or making the course of study so simple that it is devoid of opportunities for the appropriate struggle that can lead to self-efficacy.

When students with learning needs are discussed, the topics of fair assessment and grading are never far behind. The following question is most often posed: "Is it fair to grade students differently from other students just because they have an IEP or an Accommodation Plan that specifies alternative grading procedures?" The answer is simple. Not only is it fair, it is the only legal option that teachers have. If accommodations are sound, that is, they are based on documented need and supported by evidence that they yield growth, then students are assessed with accommodations in place and the student is evaluated. All students take tests and quizzes, and engage in performance tasks to demonstrate what they know, understand, and are able to do. Some teachers handle

FIGURE 4.8. CURRICULUM MODIFICATION LADDER[1]

Step	Modification	Example
1. Can the student do the **same** as peers? Student is working toward the same standards as peers.	No modification needed	Student receives the whole curriculum as it is delivered to the whole class.
2. If not, can the student do the **same** as peers with accommodations?	Accommodations in place	Student is given extended time to complete objective test
3. If not, can the student do the same activity but with **modified** materials? Student is working toward mix standards—most the same as peer.	Materials adapted	Student is given a copy of the material to be memorized
4. If not, can the student do the same activity but with **modified expectations** and adapted materials? Student is working toward mixed standards—50% modified.	Content instruction differentiated and materials adapted	Student uses prepared notes, graphic organizers to match information correctly on tests, writes a one-paragraph essay

1 Adapted from BeBoer-Haller, *Project Dakota Outreach,* Tailor Made Intervention Training and Consultation Services, as presented by Pam Schoessler and Helen Conahan-Dettrey, Chester County Intermediate Unit, September 15, 1998.

Step	Modification	Example
5. If not, can the student do a **similar** activity? Student is working toward mixed standards—80% modified.	Objective changed (fewer or different) with short bridges to the curriculum	Student orally reports 10 facts
6. If not, can the student do a similar activity but with adapted materials? Student is working toward an **alternative standard**.	Objective changed and materials changed with short bridges to the curriculum—IEP goals in place	Student produces a visual of an historic event to share with the class
7. If not, can the student do a different, **parallel** activity or product?	IEP goals	Student participates in a group research project as the materials organizer
8. If not, can the student do a **different** activity in a different section of the room?	IEP goals with setting adaptation	Student uses a computer game to match words to pictures
9. If not, can the student do a **functional** activity in a different section of the school?	IEP goals with location adaptation	Student delivers attendance bulletin to classroom teachers
10. If not, can the student be educated in the mainstream?	Location changed	Student is educated in a separate facility

the fairness question by adapting individual grading criteria and assigning separate grades for process and product. For the most part, teachers who accept the diversity of their students, with or without special needs, are more likely to give *all* students the tools they need to learn and the varied opportunities to accurately demonstrate what they have learned.

Some teachers feel compelled to report, in some way, that the course of study they deliver has been altered and no longer represents the high standards with which they typically deliver instruction. These teachers want clarifying statements included with "inflated" grades that somehow convey that the student with learning needs really didn't work as hard as the other students. Legally, the only time a district *may* consider putting such a clarifying statement on a report card is if the course has been modified for the student. Simple accommodations need not be explained on the report card. They have been explained on the IEP and in the 504 Service Agreement. Furthermore, it is discriminatory to designate on a transcript that a student has learning needs or that the curriculum was modified in some way for the student. The focus of assessment is to measure growth and communicate that growth to the student, the student's parents, and other teachers.

Because good teaching requires it, educators must develop multiple ways of assessing growth within the curricula. One such method of gathering assessment information is called Curriculum-Based Assessments (CBA). The method is called CBA because the assessments are based specifically on the objectives from the curriculum itself. CBAs are teacher-constructed criterion-referenced instruments designed to reflect progress within the curriculum. The data collected by CBAs provide a picture of the degree to which a student is using the concepts and skills taught in a curricula. During the development of a CBA, the focus is on the most critical skills and content of the curricula. During CBA construction, the teacher reexamines the major objectives in the curriculum. CBAs allow an analysis of student performance within a much broader range of normal (Tucker, 1985).

CBAs are also extremely useful for reporting progress within the general education curriculum during the special education referral or review process. The Special Education Process Chart with Time Lines (Figure 4.9) makes it possible to see when during the evaluation process, CBAs are appropriate. Steps G and H include collecting information about a student's progress within the general curricula. CBAs are diagnostic teaching tools that place emphasis on how students learn and the strategies they use rather than only the final content product of traditional summative evaluations (Conti-D'Antonio, Bertrando, & Eisenberger, 1998). Most teachers traditionally used CBAs when determining the starting point for instruction. In heterogeneous classes, at any point in the instructional process, some students may need guided practice, some may need to accelerate, and some may need additional direct instruction. CBAs have been used by teachers to determine who those learners might be and when it is necessary to adjust instruction.

FIGURE 4.9. SPECIAL EDUCATION PROCESS CHART WITH TIME LINES

Phase I—**Child Find**   Districts have a duty to seek out and find students in need of special education

| A Public Awareness | → | B Instructional Support Team | → | C Thought to be Eligible | → | D Referral Process |

Phase II—**Evaluation**

Conduct and complete an individual educational evaluation (IEE) and deliver the Comprehensive Educational Report (CER) to the parents and the team.

{- - - 45 school days - - - - - - - -10 - - - - - - - - - - - - -5 - - - - - - - - - - - - - - - - - -}

E →	F →	G &	H →
Permission to Evaluate & Procedural Safeguards are given to parents	Consent or not ready to consent:	Multidisciplinary team is established (people) MDT	Multidisciplinary evaluation is conducted (process) MDE
or	—prehearing conference		
Permission to Re-evaluate & Procedural Safeguards are given to parents	—object: Stop schedule:	CER (document)	
	—informal meeting		
(Process starts here for currently enrolled exceptional students)	—mediation		
	—prehearing conference		

(Figure continues on next page.)

Phase III—**Development of an Individual Education Program (IEP)**

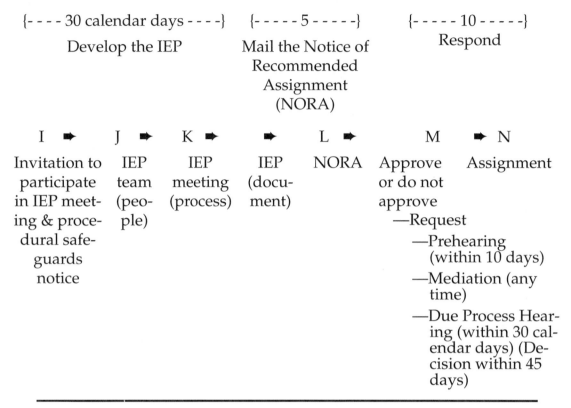

{- - - - 30 calendar days - - - -}	{- - - - - 5 - - - - -}	{- - - - 10 - - - - -}
Develop the IEP	Mail the Notice of Recommended Assignment (NORA)	Respond

I ➡	J ➡	K ➡	➡	L ➡	M	➡ N

Invitation to participate in IEP meeting & procedural safeguards notice	IEP team (people)	IEP meeting (process)	IEP (document)	NORA	Approve or do not approve
					—Request
					  —Prehearing (within 10 days)
					  —Mediation (any time)
					  —Due Process Hearing (within 30 calendar days) (Decision within 45 days)
						Assignment

CBAs are powerful learning tools for students to use to increase their knowledge and skills and/or to grapple with the obstacles they experience as they attempt to apply new knowledge and skills. Students need accurate information about their status in classes to begin the process of reflection. The process begins when the student accurately assesses his or her status in a class and then sets goals to follow. Meaningful assessment is one of the keys to student success in a school where the education of all students is a priority. What assessment methods are used, when they are used, and for what purpose they are used provide opportunities to discuss success, failure, and growth toward the self-efficacy of students with learning needs. Assessment is the basis for some of the instructional decisions educators make about students. Evaluation is the process of reflecting on all of the data collected and judging growth in comparison to curriculum expectations or expected standards.

Using CBAs to guide instruction provides an opportunity to use the Curricular Cycle—Learning to Learn (Figure 4.10) by providing students with information about their current knowledge and the skill base needed to take more self-efficacious action.

FIGURE 4.10. THE CURRICULAR CYCLE—LEARNING TO LEARN

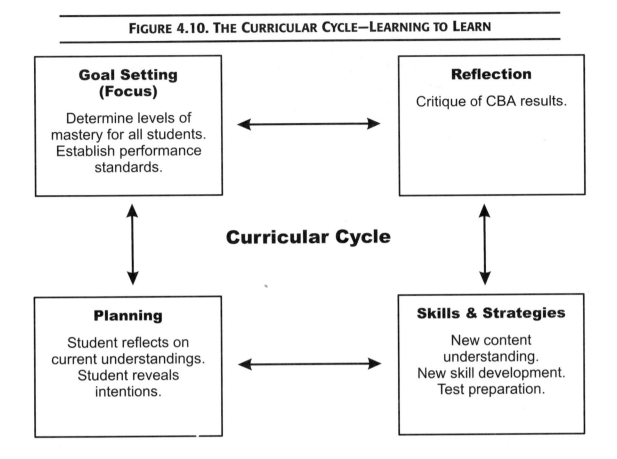

Assessments yield information that can make schools inclusionary places where growth is possible for all students. Assessments provide information that allow schools to determine which children are outside the perceived band of normal. Teachers determine whether students have mastered skills and content through assessments. Teachers establish who needs more practice and who needs enrichment in any given area as a result of assessment.

If there is a positive spin to be spun, it is that it is possible to learn the sound, best practice from the professionals in the field of special education. The strategies that have been used successfully with special needs students can be used to enhance learning for all students. For example, diagnostic teaching, a special education practice, is now shared with general education and frequently called ongoing formative assessment.

All teachers will be asked to assess students in terms of their progress in the general education curriculum. They may be asked to assess students while a student is being considered for special education or to assess the progress the exceptional students are making while included in the regular education class for instruction. And they will most certainly be required to assess the progress all students are making toward the national content standards.

Because curriculum is basic to educational assessment, CBAs provide the basis for making instructional decisions. Curriculum is the basis used to identify the gaps that occur between what the student is learning and the curriculum standard and learning goals to be met. CBAs do not necessarily yield scores and are not to be collapsed into student performance grades, but, rather provide rich information about the progress students are making within the curriculum. One such CBA, shown in Figure 4.11, was designed by a ninth-grade science teacher as a check on behavior during small group activity.

FIGURE 4.11. A CURRICULUM-BASED ASSESSMENT FOR CHECKING BEHAVIOR

Skill Behaviors for Group Activities	*Student Names*										
1. Starts to work quickly											
2. Talks in an appropriate tone											
3. Stays on task											
4. Participates without prompting											
5. Shares ideas and materials											
6. Takes turns talking											
7. Criticizes or corrects without personal attacks											
8. Defends ideas without personal attacks											

Developed by Robert Cont-D'Antonio and Joanne Eisenberger. Reproduced by permission.

The following characteristics of CBAs provide strong rationale for using them to assess progress within general education curriculum:

♦ CBAs are relevant because students are tested on what is taught.

♦ CBAs are less limited than standardized testing. Standardized tests are often out of sync with school curricula. The norming pool is restricted and therefore has a limited use for helping teachers meet the daily instructional needs of all students. Curricula is discussed at the local level, and decisions about what to include in instruction may not be addressed through national standardized assessments.

♦ CBAs address inclusion mandates. Educators address different developmental rates of learning in one class. Teachers determine if gaps are the result of lack of instruction.

♦ CBAs allow for immediate intervention. Teachers determine curricular interventions quickly.

♦ CBAs provide teachers and students with vehicles for reflection. Teachers and students reflect and share in the assessment process.

The potential for frustration and boredom exists in every teacher's classroom. The decisions made to determine the sequences with which to begin instruction, when to reinstruct and provide guided practice, and when to provide enrichment are the most critical yet challenging decisions teachers make. Choosing where to begin instruction is the first step in providing instruction to a broader range of students. CBAs can assist the teacher in that first step. This type of formative assessment has been referred to as "providing a window of learning" (Tucker, 1985) for kid watching. Students benefit best from instruction that is at their independent level of learning, but that still requires a degree of rigor and appropriate challenge.

Providing learning tasks that support optimum growth is a goal of CBAs. CBAs are tools for "dipsticking." Dipsticking is the moment during instruction when teachers purposefully check for what students know, understand, and are able to do (Conti-D'Antonio, Bertrando, & Eisenberger, 1998). Differentiating instruction, based on these decisions is critical to offset frustration and boredom and to provide the education experiences that support rigorous learning and growth toward self-efficacy.

Typically, the steps to developing and using CBAs to guide instruction follow this plan:[2]

♦ Select sample critical items from curricula or write some curricula items to match the curricula. Be sure both *content and process* are included.

♦ Order the skill/content by difficulty. Write an objective for each.

♦ Prepare items to test each objective. Administer.

♦ Construct two more similar tests (tests #2 and #3).

♦ Administer tests #2 and #3 on different days. This step can be eliminated if validity is not an issue).

---

2 Adapted from Blankenship (1985) and Idol (1986).

◆ Test fluency (both speed and accuracy). Record all student responses. Performance criteria could be established to determine levels of mastery in a collaborative way between the special education teacher and the regular education teacher. In other words, decide what excellent, good, and emerging work will look like.

◆ Ask these questions:
  • Which students have mastered the objective?
  • Which students possess sufficient prerequisite skill to begin instruction on the objective?
  • Which students lack mastery of prerequisite skill to begin instruction on the objective?

◆ Readminister CBA after instruction. Study the answers to these questions:
  • Which students have mastered the skills and are ready to begin instruction on a new topic?
  • Which students have acquired the topic but require more practice to achieve mastery?
  • Which students are making insufficient progress, thereby requiring the teacher to adapt some aspect of instruction?

Because process is just as important as content when making assessments, when creating CBAs, the real challenge is to name the skills along with the content that students must know, understand, and be able to do. A social studies list would look like the following after the teacher attended to skills and processes:

◆ Name and describe the memorization strategies you use to recall the facts of this unit.

◆ Compare an event from the past with one from the present and explain the similarities.

◆ Write a topic sentence with supporting details and a conclusion statement.

◆ Identify key points in a text about a specific topic.

◆ Categorize information for presentation.

◆ Orally compose the summary.

To employ CBAs means to use material being taught as a basis for assessing the degree to which it has been learned (Tucker, 1985). CBAs can provide very sophisticated, yet practical data that can be used during the process for identifying students in need of remediation and enrichment. CBAs can also be used to measure success within the educational system specifically by analyzing the students' progress in the curriculum of the local school. Of course, gauging this degree of achievement can happen only when the expected curricular outcomes are known and measurable (Tucker, 1985). Teachers are most often expert in identifying the content goals of their courses. They can be heard saying: "At the end of the unit, my kids will be able to combine fractions with unlike denominators...." "Describe how the mitochondria function...." "Tell how to determine a telling sentence from an asking sentence."

For example, a high school social studies teacher was asked to identify the skills/processes that he knew were critical for a student to be successful in his ninth-grade Western Civilization units. The teacher developed the following list:

♦ Memorize 50 facts.

♦ Design a visual that represents a historical event that parallels modern society.

♦ Compose a one-paragraph essay comparing or contrasting a historic to a modern event. (The paragraph must include a thesis sentence, three supporting detail sentences, and a conclusion.)

♦ Research, compile, and present a 10-minute elaboration about an event or concept from the time period being studied.

Rates of acquisition and retention of new learning are determined based on progress in the general education curriculum. The point at which the student learns comfortably is of primary importance. The data collected should be aimed at information related to supporting the child to be involved in and progress through the general curriculum. Decisions about placement into special education programs are often made after collecting this kind of data and combining it with data taken from a standardized assessment vehicle.

> Example: Curricular goal: Student will increase reading fluency. 1.1 grade level text was used; student read 45 words/minute with four errors. After 10 weeks of instruction, the following data are collected: 52 words/minute with 3 errors (2 words/minute correct/week with 4 errors) Retention was also poor in that the student maintained the same level of comprehension.

Another way to examine students' progress within the general curriculum is by looking at the time it takes them to learn. Academic Learning Time, as the formula in Figure 4.12 shows, is the amount of time students spend in relevant content that they can perform at high success (Borg, 1980).

**FIGURE 4.12. FORMULA FOR DETERMINING ACADEMIC LEARNING TIME
(FROM THOMPSON, GICKLING, & HAVERTAPE, 1983)**

Time on task—The % of time the student is actually engaged in the task-related behavior.

Task completion—The number of items attempted, whether right or wrong, are counted. The number of attempts is divided by the number required by the task.

Task comprehension—Each task item understood is counted by directly questioning the student. The number of correct answers is divided by total questions asked.

Academic Learning Time—Add the three numbers from the calculations above.

Some teachers may be more familiar with analyzing student performance in terms of levels of performance rather than in terms of Academic Learning Time. Individual Reading Inventories (IRI) or Individual Math Inventories (IMI) are examples of assessment devices that can provide the teacher with levels of performance within the general curriculum. The following examples are scales of CBAs:

Reading Levels	*Math Levels*
Independent Reading: 93–97% accuracy	Independent Application and Problem Solving: 85–100% accuracy
Instructional drill: 70–85% accuracy	Instructional drill: 70–85% accuracy
Frustration: less than 70% accuracy	Frustration: less than 70% accuracy

Instructional tasks presented in CBAs are selected in terms of the type of task, the number of items in the task, the ratio of known to unknown that translates to performance levels, and the student's performance of the task. General guidelines are followed when using CBAs. The process need not be a cumbersome one. The following common sense procedures can help:

♦ It's helpful to record student behavior in different settings. For example, teachers should consider assessing in two or more of the following settings:

whole-group instruction labs   small cooperative groups centers

individual work   remedial

enrichment   tutorial

- Start slowly. For example:

    focus on one skill

    focus on one or two children

    focus during independent work time

    focus on small group rather than whole class

- A variety of CBAs can be developed focusing on a variety of specific skills in different content contexts. Consider these contexts:

composing	attention
memorizing	questioning
researching	spontaneous language generation
on/off taskness	reading for main idea
working with precision	fluency (speed + accuracy)
metacognition	self-advocacy
constructing for meaning	self-efficacy

- Consider the ways in which the student best learns. Some examples follow:

oral rehearsal	peer tutoring
goal setting	high structure
concrete manipulation	

At the upper levels of middle school, junior high school, and high school, well-constructed rubrics, content and process tests, portfolios, demonstrations, verbal responses that allow for fuller understanding of the student's thinking process, and checklists can form the basis for assessing progress within the general curriculum and can be made into useful CBAs. Math and reading scope and sequence guides, if they are valid representations of the instruction that occurs in the general curriculum, also provide starting points for developing CBAs. Rubrics clarify performance expectations and provide a shared guide for the teacher and student as they work through the assessment process. Rubrics can also be used as very effective CBAs.

Good classroom management is essential during "kid watching." Teachers need to remain acutely aware of what is happening in all parts of the classroom at all times, intervening promptly with suggestions and nonverbal cues. Teachers need to respond to individuals while keeping the whole group on task. Effective classroom managers exhibit these key teacher behaviors:

- With-it-ness—remaining aware of what is happening in all parts of the classroom

♦ Overlapping—being able to do more than one thing at a time; providing fast-paced lessons that use signals rather than distracting verbal prompts to sustain momentum

♦ Differentiating instruction and providing instruction focused at the correct level of difficulty (Kounin, 1970)

For more information on management, see Chapter 2.

A seasoned teacher will immediately ask about the strategies that can be used to manage the amount of information that can potentially be collected on students during class time. The following 5 x 7 note card strategy is used by Donna Blakeman, peer coach with Unionville Chadds Ford School District:

> Use masking tape to put cards semipermanently on the insides of a manila folder. The cards should overlap so that approximately 10 cards can go on each side of the folder. Tape the cards onto the folder along the lower side of the card. Student names are written on the corners of the cards. As teachers circulate and kid watch, they note critical information on the respective cards about each student. As a card fills, it is peeled from the folder and put directly in the student's file. The teacher does not have to recopy the information, saving valuable time while providing a solid basis for reporting out to parents, teachers, and the students themselves about the progress each student has made within the general curriculum.

In summary, when using CBAs:

♦ Focus on what students CAN do.

♦ Emphasize what students LEARNED, not what was taught.

♦ Broaden the range of what is considered normal. (Students progress through developmental stages, not discrete, easily measured points in time.)

♦ Consider these descriptors that can be used consistently when assessing how students are managing new material: "not yet," "with guidance," "beginning to," and "independently."

Figure 4.13 is an example of a CBA used by a teacher to guide her instruction. Additional reproducible CBAs are provided in Appendix II: Forms. Remember that students do not always make the growth that is anticipated. Even with Accommodation Plans and IEPs in place, students fail. This disappointment is the perfect opportunity for reflection and assessment of the obstacles and facilitators of the student's current progress. When self-efficacy and independence are a part of a learner's program, poor school performance can provide the context for goal setting and growth.

FIGURE 4.13. A CURRICULUM-BASED ASSESSMENT BASED ON BLOOM'S TAXONOMY (ADAPTED FROM THE UNIONVILLE HIGH SCHOOL THINKING SKILLS PROJECT)

Date _12/6/99_ Grade _11_ Subject _U.S. Culture_ Teacher _C-D_

Through 12/13/99—end of unit evaluation

Indicator	Always (5)	Usually (4)	Some-times (3)	Occa-sionally (2)	Not Yet (1)	Not Ap-plicable (0)	Comments, Observations, Evidence
Perserverance	5	4	③	2	1	0	cuing regularly —not independent
Decreased impulsivity	5	④	3	2	1	0	good questions
Flexibility	⑤	4	3	2	1	0	listening to each other
Metacognition	5	4	3	②	1	0	annoyed when they had to start
Careful review	5	4	③	2	1	0	most spent time polishing and
Problem posing	5	4	③	2	1	0	considering carefully
Past knowledge	5	④	3	2	1	0	pulled in knowledge from first
Enjoyment of problem solving	5	④	3	2	1	0	unit, seemed to be linking knowledge
Precise language	5	4	3	②	1	0	still too much slang

(Figure continues on next page.)

include in grade
next to unit

CHARACTERISTIC	DESCRIPTION	BEHAVIOR	CUES/PROMPTS
Perseverance	Working until solution is reached	Tries again, debates strategy, changes strategies	Look at this again. What else might you try?
Decreased impulsivity	Pausing to reflect or clarify, requesting more information	Asks for facts, pauses before answering	Speed doesn't count. Gather your thoughts. Take your time.
Flexibility	Considering the other points of view, trying new approaches	Paraphrases others, accepts suggestions or directions, evaluates responses	Can anyone think of another way to… Let's try looking at this another way.
Metacognition	Analyzing, describing one's own thought processes	Retraces steps, describes strategies and processes used	Go through the steps aloud. How did you do that?
Careful review	Proofing work, comparing work to criteria or exemplar	Reflects on accuracy of work, checks to ensure accuracy	Did you compare your work to the rubric? Have you used a peer editor?
Problem posing	Asking questions and finding problems to solve	Wonders. Asks for proof or evidence	How do you know? What would happen if…?
Past knowledge	Using prior knowledge or past learning	Makes connection to past experience, content or ideas	Does this remind you of anything else? Where else might this be useful?
Enjoyment of problem solving	Solving problems with increasing joy and independence	Positive comments. On task for extended period of time.	You're doing great. Keep working. I'm pleased to see you're hanging in there.
Precise language	Using appropriate descriptive words and labels	Uses analogies, complete sentences Concise.	Stop and think[3] first. What is the scientific word for that?

strategy for
next unit
see Joanna E for more

---

3 For additional information on the Stop and Think process, see Appendix I: Strategies.

REFERENCES

Bertrando, R., Conti-D'Antonio, M., & Eisenberger, J. (1992). *Unionville High School Thinking Skills Project: Final Report.* Kennett Square, PA: Unionville Chadds Ford School District.

Blankenship, C. (1985). Using curriculum based assessment data to make instructional decisions. *Exceptional Children, 52,* 233–238.

Blakeman, D. (1998). *IDEA Training.* Kennet Square, PA: Unionville Chadds Ford School District.

Borg, W. R. (1980). *Time and School Learning. Time to Learn.* Washington, DC: US Department of Education.

Conti-D'Antonio, M., Bertrando, R., & Eisenberger, J. (1998). *Supporting Students with Learning Needs in the Block.* Larchmont, NY: Eye On Education.

Faust, A. (1998). *IDEA '97 Training.* Presented at Intermediate Unit # 24, August 27, 1998. Exton, PA.

Gickling, E., & Thompson, V. (1985). A personal view of curriculum-based assessment. *Exceptional Children, 52 (3),* 205–218.

Hill, B., Ruptic, C., & Norwick, L. (1998). *Classroom-Based Assessment.* Norwood, MA: Christopher Gorden.

Idol, L. (1986). *Models of Curriculum-Based Assessment.* Pro-ed.

Kounin, G. (1970). Discipline and group management in classrooms. In Brophy, J. (1996). *Teaching Problem Students* (pp. 10–11). New York: Holt, Rinehart & Winston.

Leo, J. (1998, October 20). *Let's Lower the Bar.* www.usnews.com.

Salend, S. J. (1995). Treatment acceptability: Determining appropriate interventions within inclusive classrooms. *Intervention in School and Clinic, 31,* 84–90.

Sammons, R., & Davey, B. (1994, December/January). Textbook awareness and performance profile. *Journal of Reading 37*(4), 280–286.

Schoesler, P. (1998). *Individuals with Disabilities Education Act, Amendments of 1997: Level II Implementation Training.* Exton, PA: Chester County Intermediate Unit, Eastern Instructional Support Center, Pennsylvania Department of Education.

Thompson, V. P., Gickling, E. E., & Havertape, J. F. (1983). The effects of medication and curriculum on task-related behaviors of attention deficit disordered and low achieving peers. *Monographs in Behavior Disorders: Severe Behavior Disorders of Children and Youth* Series #6. CCBD, Tuscon, AZ.

Thurlow, M. L., Elliot, J. L., Ysseldyke, J. E. (1998). *Testing Students with Disabilities: Practical Strategies for Complying with District and State Requirements.* Thousand Oaks, CA: Corwin Press.

Tucker, J. (1985). Curriculum based assessment: An introduction. *Exceptional Children, 52 (3)*, 199–204.

5

WORKING
WITH PARENTS

No other school settings provide parents, teachers and students with the opportunity to come together to solve problem as frequently as parent conferences. Teachers and administrators, carried by the tide of the day's activities, rarely come together for the explicit purpose of decision making for the benefit of one child outside the parent conference. Parents rarely have a window into how teachers and administrators problem solve the demands placed on education, even though those decisions have a direct effect on the success or failure of school as it relates to their children. All schools have in them a wide variety of well-meaning professionals who speak earnestly about *helping* students. However, systems and people who support efficacious behavior are not always seen as champions of the student. "Well meaning adults stack the emotional deck for themselves, often unconsciously, by establishing roles in their school relationships that assure they will get the psychic strokes they need" (Landfried, 1989, pp. 61–65). People who embrace self-efficacy must acknowledge that not all those making decisions about the learner share their philosophy about independence.

The goal for parent meetings is to make good decisions about what is best for the learner. These meetings can be land mines of highly charged, intense discussions involving parents or guardians who may be emotionally strained. "Conference participants must be reminded that the setbacks children endure serve a beneficial purpose in teaching that success usually requires sustained effort" (Bandura, 1997, p. 245). During the conference, it's important to clarify goals and to use language that all participants understand. There may be philosophical differences among the people meeting. For example, during conferences, participants often discuss "helping" the learner. Care must be taken to recognize how much of a detriment one connotation of the word "help" may be, in the long run, to independence. A parent or unenlightened professional may define "help" as minimizing rigor and standards, when the student needs to be taught ways to deal with rigor and high standards. Depending on the concerns and problems that surface during a conference, psychiatric or psychological counseling may provide the necessary support that some parents may need to identify the less obvious, but just as challenging, social and emotional issues facing students with learning needs (Lerner, 1971).

Successful students usually have parent advocates. The key is to keep the advocacy positive so that parents remain supportive rather than combative toward the school. This advocacy is particularly strong among parents of students with learning needs. These were the parents who provided the impetus to stimulate research, legislation, and the expansion of special education public law in the late 1960s and 1970s (Schmidt & Foster, 1976) that ultimately led to the 1997 reauthorization of the Individuals with Disabilities Education Act (IDEA). Educators should not be surprised with the level of involvement parents of students with learning needs continue to display.

During parent conferences, the focus must remain on the student's progress so that setbacks set the stage for self-efficacy development. Although the happiness and self-esteem of the student are important concerns, these attributes must not become the focus of the conference. All of the conference participants may need to be reminded that developing efficacy requires experience in over-coming obstacles through effort.

Teachers must be aware that parents enter conferences with many intense emotional issues. Parents not only need to accept the problems of having a child with learning needs, but also must accept that progress toward academic, so-cial, and self-efficacy goals could be slow or at least be different from the goals of other children. Parents' reactions to having a child with learning needs are similar to the developmental stages dealing with grief: deny the problem exists, become angry, search for another diagnosis, and accept the challenge. Because of these parental attitudes, a teacher must enter parent meetings well prepared. It is critical that the educators remain focused, professional, and calm.

The literature is full of good solid tips for general parent conferencing (Can-ter & Canter, 1991; Clement, 1997). Most of the discussion centers on methods for establishing rapport, maintaining privacy, encouraging active participation, problem solving, and goal setting. Conferencing with parents of students who have serious learning needs requires careful structure and specific goals. School professionals will be expected to share the instructional adaptations that were tried and found to be engaging and effective. All parties will be expected to de-scribe the strengths and weaknesses of the learner. Parents will be expected to discuss the expectations they have for their children, as well as how those ex-pectations could be achieved. Parents also bear the special privilege of being the child's first teachers. It is important that all participants respect each other's voices.

Dealing more effectively with parents of children with learning needs re-quires teachers to follow guidelines based on sound research as well as best-practice methods. Participation in an Individual Education Plan (IEP) meeting requires that all involved accomplish the specific tasks required by the IDEA Federal Law. Participation, when developing a Service Plan, which is an agree-ment between the education agency and the student who qualifies for accom-modations under Section 504 of the Rehabilitation Act of 1973, can be just as complex. The individual members of the decision-making team should be pre-pared to problem solve with a group whose members may have very different views on what is best for children and what encompasses best educational prac-tice. Focus must be fixed on the steps that are necessary to facilitate independ-ence for the learner; individual egos and personal needs must be secondary concerns.

All participants involved in planning for students should be wary of indi-viduals who want to make themselves indispensable to students. If students perceive their success to be impossible without a specific adult intervention, then a student's road to self-efficacy will be detoured by well meaning, albeit, personally needy adults. Consider what Bandura lists in *Self-Efficacy: The Exer-cise of Control* (1997, pp. 244–247) (Figure 5.1) and the effect teachers' beliefs in their efficacy has toward their general orientation toward educational pro-cesses, as well as toward instructional activities.

FIGURE 5.1. TEACHERS' EFFICACY BELIEFS

High Efficacy Beliefs	*Low Efficacy Beliefs*
Optimism about their ability to teach and reach a wide population of students.	Pessimism about their ability to influence student behavior and enhance students' motivation.
Confidence that difficult students are reachable and teachable through extra effort and appropriate techniques.	Distrust in their ability to manage the classroom. Stressed and angered by student misbehavior.
Actively enlist family supports.	Contact parents only for punitive sanctions.
Work to overcome community influences through effective teaching.	Use negative sanctions to get students to work. Mired in classroom problems.
Believe efficacy is an accurate prediction of student achievement.	Use strict regulation for classroom management and learning.
Enjoy their profession and express satisfaction with their job.	Take a custodial view of their job and if they had to do it again, would not choose the profession.

It is truly a paradigm shift for some people to think about students as potentially efficacious and independent. This shift in thinking requires a certain conscious effort to communicate as clearly as possible, as often as possible, and to all who will listen that standards and rigor are important for all learners, that appropriate strategies can be taught to learners, and that support doesn't mean enabling. A clearly articulated learning plan that includes a cycle of goal setting, planning, skill and strategy instruction, and reflection is critical. The parent conference provides an appropriate entry point into the cycle of learning at the goal setting, planning, or reflection stages. (See Chapter 3 for more information about exercises that support efficacious behavior.)

Consider Figure 2.10 (pp. 32–36) (a chart that details problem student types, indicators, teacher behaviors, and student strategies, which was compiled from the work of Lynn Meltzer (1992) and Jere Brophy (1996)) as a resource when planning for conferences. The chart facilitates the teacher's problem solving as it relates to determining the problems student have and the strategies available to the teacher to begin addressing those problems.

Parents, too, have very specific responsibilities as they relate to their child's success in school. Efficacious schools involve parents as partners. Educators should encourage parents to foster self-efficacy in their children by exhibiting these behaviors:

- Place a value on education
- Set beliefs about scholastic abilities
- Establish regular homework habits
- Set standards of excellence
- Help with school work at home
- Keep track of academic progress
- Support school related functions
- Assist with school activities
- Reward efforts
- Prepare children for school (Bandura, 1997, pp. 244–247)

Parents need to see and hear evidence during parent conferences that students are learning within a system that supports the highest level of student independence. The teacher's responsibility is to assist the learner as the learner moves through the goal setting, planning, learning skills and strategies, and reflection stages. Students need to know that they will be taught strategies for reflecting on successes as well as failures, strategies for goal setting and planning, and strategies for managing new information and skills. Students will learn how to set high goals and reach them by using systematic application of learning strategies.[1] This contrasts with what typically goes on in special education classes where "teachers spend significant amounts of time helping students complete homework assignments, study for tests, or clarify content from their general education classes" (Hughes, 1999, p. 5). At best, this is a short-term tutorial that serves to make people feel good. It results in little lasting impact on the student except to ensure dependence on tutoring.

The following guidelines for planning before the conference, maintaining focus during the conference, and concluding the conference provide a good structure to follow to ensure that the critical components of teaching for self-efficacy are discussed with the parents.

BEFORE THE CONFERENCE

Take time before the conference to write down the specific points that will be made and gather the documentation to support those points. For example, the student is well served if the teacher takes the time to discuss the practical differences between the two concepts of self-esteem and self-efficacy. Teachers must make clear to parents what classroom practice looks like and sounds like if a position of self-efficacy is embraced.

- Find out who will be involved in the conference and decide whether others should be invited. Will the parents come alone? Will they bring a local child advocate? Might they bring an attorney? Who

---

1   For explanations of specific learning strategies, see Appendix I: Strategies.

does the teacher want involved? Should the teacher ask the guidance person or the principal to attend? If the teacher believes the parents will exercise their due process rights and request a due process hearing, the teacher may want the special education supervisor involved.

♦ Gather information from a variety of sources. Check on attendance. Read the student's discipline record. Meet with the nurse to ascertain information about health issues and medication. Speak with other teachers about the student's progress within the general curriculum. Determine how the student is managing material, retaining information, and applying the new information. Does the student sustain effort when faced with setbacks and difficult tasks? For example, one of the more effective ways of gathering information, *The Accommodation Checklist,*[2] assists the observer in categorizing the types of supports the learner needs in the areas of presentation, response, setting, instruction, scheduling, assistive devices, and motivation.

♦ Plan positive comments to say during the conference. Consider comments that address social, emotional physical, creative, and intellectual areas. Make a statement that addresses the student's control over academic tasks by the student's use of strategies. Use the "sandwich" technique: If you must say something negative, sandwich the negative statement between two positive statements.

♦ Plan to discuss the strategies that are currently being used or the anticipated strategies that will allow the student to perform with greater success. For example, if the teacher anticipates speaking about the student's current limited ability to focus and remain attentive, the teacher should plan to demonstrate a strategy such as "Chairs in Place" or "The Attention Tape" (Conti-D'Antonio, Bertrando, & Eisenberger, 1998).[3]

♦ Be prepared to discuss the difference between self-esteem and self-efficacy and the strategies that support self-efficacy. A parent may not know that self-efficacy is "the belief in one's capabilities to organize and execute the courses of action required to manage perspective situations" (Bandura, 1986, p. 391) or that self-concept is simply the way a person describes herself. A teacher may need to tell a parent that self-esteem is the evaluation of that self-concept and comes from how the person feels about himself (Pope, McHale, & Crud, 1988), and that the self-assurance with which people approach a

---

2 See Appendix II: Forms.

3 For an explanation of these strategies, see Appendix I: Strategies.

difficult task determines whether they make good or poor use of their abilities.

♦ Make a general outline of the conference and practice the "script." Oral rehearsal can build the fluency and confidence that is critical if a teacher is to be respected and seen as a resource to the learner and his family. Set high goals for the conference outcomes.

♦ Prepare to address some the topics that parents frequently ask. Parents of children with learning needs often have very specific questions to ask the school district during a conference. Parents are often coached by advocacy groups or they have read booklets and pamphlets about their rights under the law. They will come prepared with questions such as these:

  • What special skills does my child need to improve?

  • Does my child have difficulty in one class or all classes?

  • What teaching methods work best for my child?

  • What methods have you tried?

  • How long have they been in place?

  • Should the child spend more or less time in the general curriculum? (Mancuso, Reiser, & Stotland, 1991, p. 19)

♦ Regardless of how much coaching a parent has received, the teacher is still the professional. The teacher is the single most influential person in the student's educational life; the teacher is the most important factor in determining student achievement (Wong, 1999). It is crucial for the professionals to keep the focus on self-efficacy and what it means for the student. Teachers must apply these requirements when planning for instruction for all students:

  • Rigor will occur in incremental stages to match the skills and strategies the student is learning.

  • Students will learn to embrace challenge and persist through challenging tasks.

  • Tasks will be rigorous and engaging. (Csikszentmihalyi, Rathunde, & Whalen, 1993, pp. 177–196).

♦ Prepare the student if the student is to participate in the conference. Discuss the events that are likely to occur during the meeting. Help the student structure some of his or her thoughts. If the student attends the conference, the student will be asked to contribute, and will need oral rehearsal opportunities if he or she is to contribute and benefit from the experience.

♦ The teacher must consider everything that has led up to the conference. An analysis of this information is important if the teacher is to make insightful contributions during the meeting.

♦ Use the sample plan in Figure 5.2 to assist you during the planning stage.

FIGURE 5.2. A TEACHER PLANS FOR A PARENT CONFERENCE

CONFERENCE PLAN/REPORT

Before the meeting:

Agenda	Meeting date/time/place	Participants
Review Joey John's progress at the request of his parents	5/6/99 11:35 guidance suite	Mr. Johns (father) Mrs. Johns (mother) Joey Johns (student) Miss Conti (special ed) Mr. Beard (psych) Mr. Betrando (general ed)
	Materials Student's Goal-Setting Pyramid, Skill Evaluation and Assignment Notebook	

Teacher's Positive Theme	Teacher's Strategy/Suggestion
Identify recent successes Discuss growth (not grades) and improved attendance Describe student's ability to reflect and take responsibility	Identify strategies that work Discuss difference between self-esteem and self-efficacy Identify self-efficacy markers

---

DURING THE CONFERENCE

Teachers who teach for self-efficacy don't enable. During the conference, teachers must be prepared to give concrete examples of what self-efficacious behavior will and will not look like in their classrooms. This means being clear that parents and teachers do not do tasks that are student tasks. For example:

♦ Teachers will not pick up trash left by students.

♦ Teachers will not make flimsy excuses for children to avoid criticism for lack of discipline from supervisors.

♦ Teachers will not put words in students' mouths struggling for the correct answer. (Landfried, 1989, pp. 80–81)

To prepare for the parent conference, use this checklist:

♦ Be very clear at the onset of the conference regarding what can and cannot be accomplished. A statement such as "this is what we need to have done by the end of the meeting…" provides the parents with a clear understanding of the conference goals.

♦ Take notes and stay focused. Keep the agenda moving steadily along. The teacher needs to be specific in the comments that are made, avoid jargon that only serves to confound parents, stress collaboration in planning for the student, and focus on solutions. If goals are not met during the conference, agree to meet again. Little can be accomplished if conferences go on for hours and nerves become frayed.

♦ Agree to do things that are appropriate for the teacher to do. Do not take on responsibilities that are clearly those of the student or the parents. Remember that it is the job of the teacher to teach for independence and self-efficacy. That means modeling the assumption of appropriate responsibility. There are responsibilities that are the learner's alone. They are neither the responsibilities of the parents nor of the teacher.

• Students will not be allowed to tune out while the teacher does the talking.

• Students will not be allowed to "forget" assignments without penalty.

• Students will not be given credit for sloppy work.

• Students will not cheat without penalties.

• Students will not take tests and receive grades for work that is too easy.

• Students will not be allowed to sleep, read newspapers, or carry on irrelevant conversations during class activities. (Landfried, 1989, pp. 80–81)

♦ Listen actively. Recognize that the whole picture includes a family culture with values or norms that may be foreign to you. Talk about the difference between self-esteem and self-efficacy; those concepts may be foreign, too. The student's welfare is the primary focus.

♦ Be sensitive and diplomatic. Put yourself in the shoes of a parent who is coping with a youngster who is not the perfect child they thought they had. Help them establish realistic goals. (DeBruyn, 1998)

♦ Do not try to "wing it" during a conference regarding children with learning needs. Parents are savvy about their rights and the rights of their children to free and appropriate education (FAPE). Create a framework to structure the conference. Follow these steps within the framework:

- Identify no more than two major concerns.
- Select preferred strategies for dealing with the major concerns from a brainstormed list of possible strategies.
- Confirm who is doing what. Don't forget to include the student.
- Agree when periodic reviews will occur.

♦ Do not make statements similar to, "Your child needs a tutor;" "Johnny would benefit from smaller classes;" or "The nice private school down the street works really well with learners like your daughter." Teachers must remember that they work for the school district and represent the district. Comments made in passing may be construed by parents as endorsements and approval for placements or services for which they expect the district to pay.

♦ Keep to the facts. Don't guess or make generalizations. Avoid fixing blame. These approaches are counterproductive and put the teacher's professional ability in question. (DeBruyn, 1999)

♦ When failures occur, they need to be seen as opportunities for growth rather than assessments that can be denied or bargained away. Even students armed with IEPs and accommodation plans fail. The IEP does not guarantee success. Students and their families need to accept the failure first, and then begin to work with the teacher to reflect on the obstacles that prevented success. The teacher needs to be capable of discussing the process of reflection, goal setting, planning, and skill/strategy development. For more information on this "cycle of learning," see Chapter 3.

♦ Use a closing strategy. As with good instruction, a good summary can be the difference between constructive meaning and confusion. A good ending has the potential to solidify the parent's positive perceptions of the teacher. When conferences are stressful, the only thing that the some parties might agree to is for continued meetings. In those cases, it is most important that parents know that they will be engaged in a relationship with a professional who does have strategies to share that will support their child in the path to independence and self-efficacy.

♦ Document all pertinent information collected and actions agreed upon at the conference. An example of documentation that might be used is shown in Figure 5.3.

FIGURE 5.3. A TEACHER RECORDS THE EVENTS DURING A PARENT CONFERENCE

CONFERENCE PLAN/REPORT

During the meeting:	
Parent's Needs/Goals For Joey to feel good about himself For Joey to assume more responsibility and to be more independent, to see evidence of growth	**Parent's Problems** Grades have not improved
Minutes of the Meeting Introductions were made, and parents identified problems. Teacher restated problems into goals for the conference. Joey *shared* artifacts to demonstrate his *growth*—better assessment scores. Miss Conti shared the upcoming strategy instruction that Joey will engage in, focusing on reflection, goal setting, and strategy instruction.	
Decision Miss Conti confirmed that Joey will be held accountable when he "forgets" assignments and that established teacher policies for penalties for missing work will be adhered to. Miss Conti will continue to periodically collect artifacts that she and Joey will analyze and reflect on. The documents will be summarized or duplicated and sent home to parents. The next meeting will occur on June 13, 1999.	

AFTER THE CONFERENCE

Think of the time spent after the meeting as preparation for the next conference. Review conference notes and document the problems and potential solutions to those problems (Figure 5.4). Teachers can use the list below to help structure the followup work that is necessary.

♦ List the benefits for implementing any conference suggestions. It is important to monitor and document.

♦ List the actions that will be taken. Follow-up with the parents in a brief phone call or note regarding how the actions they agreed to do during the conference are being carried out.

FIGURE 5.4. A TEACHER FOLLOWS UP ON A PARENT CONFERENCE AND PLANS FOR THE NEXT MEETING

CONFERENCE PLAN/REPORT[4]

After the meeting:		
Benefits Clarified the difference between self-esteem and self-efficacy Established common critical focus Concerns identified	**What is in the way?** Parents' expectation for fluency (speed and accuracy) may be unrealistic Joey's goals and parents' goals are different	
Next Action by Parent At home, parent will use "sandwich" technique when responding to Joey's progress in school	**Next Action by Student** Share homework assignment book with parents Explain skill evaluation to parents Complete a new goal-setting pyramid with Miss Conti	**Next Action by School** Provide skill instruction in assignment tracking

♦ Communicate to teachers, guidance counselors, and administrators. Explain the outcome of the conference. Educators must be seen as resources to the parents, the experts on their own children. The professional's responsibility is to hold up high expectations for all students and to offer ideas for parents to try that will make them partners in the process.

♦ Always do what you have agreed to do. Make the actions that are agreed to by the student part of the learning strategy instruction. Monitor and document the effects of your actions and the student's efforts in preparation for the next conference.

Parent conferences provide educators with an opportunity to discuss the philosophy and its underpinnings of self-efficacy and independence. Parent conferences demand that educators be well informed, articulate, and professional. Parent conferences are rich with opportunity and should not be minimized.

---

4 For more information on the Learning Strategies named in the Conference Plan/Report, see Appendix I: Strategies. A reproducible copy of the Conference Plan/Report is provided in Appendix II: Forms.

REFERENCES

Alley, G., & Deshler, D. (1979). *Teaching the Learning Disabled Adolescent: Strategies and Methods.* Denver, CO: Love Publishing.

Bandura, A. (1997). *Self-Efficacy: The Exercise of Control.* New York: W.H. Freeman.

Bandura, A. (1986). *Social Foundations of Thought and Action: A Social Cognitive Theory.* Englewood Cliffs, NJ: Prentice-Hall.

Brophy, J. (1996). *Teaching Problem Students.* New York: Guilford Press.

Canter, L., & Canter, M. (1991). *Parents on Your Side.* Santa Monica, CA: Lee Canter.

Clement, M. (1997). *Put Your Oxygen Mask on First.* Virginia Beach, VA: Teachers' Little Secrets.

Conti-D'Antonio, M., Bertrando, R., & Eisenberger, J. (1998). *Supporting Students with Learning Needs in the Block.* Larchmont, NY: Eye On Education.

Csikszentmihalyi, M., Rathunde, K., Whalen, S. (1993). *Talented Teenagers.* New York: Cambridge University Press.

DeBruyn, R. (1998). Seven tips for ending conversations with parents. *The Master Teacher, 30*(7), 1–6.

DeBruyn, R. (1999). Now is the time. *The Master Teacher, 30, (30).* Kansas City, MO: Leadership Lane.

Hughes, C. (1999, Spring). Helping adolescents with learning disabilities become strategic learners. *Bridges, Research into Practice.* State College, PA: College of Education, 1–5.

Landfried, S. (1989). "Enabling" undermines responsibility in students. *Educational Leadership, 47,* 79–83.

Lerner, J. (1971). *Children with Learning Disabilities.* Boston, MA: Houghton Mifflin.

Loucks, H. E., & Waggoner, J. E. (1998). *Classroom Connections: Parent-Teacher Conferences.* Columbus, OH: National Middle School Association.

Mancuso, E., Reiser, L., & Stotland, J. (1991) *The Right to Special Education in Pennsylvania: A Guide for Parents.* Philadelphia, PA: The Education Law Center.

Meltzer, L. (1992). *Strategy Use in Students with Learning Disabilities: The Challenge of Assessment, Strategy Assessment and Instruction for Students with Learning Disabilities: From Theory to Practice.* Austin, TX: Pro-Ed.

Schmidt, C., & Foster, G., (1976). *Parent and Community Involvement: Learning Disabilities Handbook.* Chicago, IL: University Press.

Pope, A. W., McHale, S. M., & Crud, W. E. (1988). *Self-Esteem Enhancement with Children and Adolescents.* New York: Pergamon.

Wong, H. (1999). *Induction: Helping Teachers Succeed on the First Days of School.* Mountain View, CA: H.K. Wong.

APPENDIX I

STRATEGIES

I CAN

The lack of self-efficacy often limits a student's ability to respond creatively to situations and challenges. To be successful in academic tasks, students need to believe in their ability to achieve. The I Can strategy provides a process for re-training negative self-defeating internal dialogues (I can't), to positive and more helpful (I can) thoughts. Students should be taught the dialogue process during a time of calm and then be cued to use the set of questions when the negative thoughts intrude. Students will need some skill training in rephrasing negative thought to positives before using this strategy in a stressful situation.

STEPS

1. Think of an "I can't" statement that you often make and write it down.

2. Below the statement, list as many thoughts and fears as you can associate with it.

3. Ask and answer these questions:
   • What is a different or more helpful way I can think?
   • How does the new helpful thought make me feel?
   • Is it helpful to keep thinking the new thought? Why or why not?

4. Rephrase the original statement into an "I can" statement.

Some students find it useful to associate a physical "trigger" (snap of the fingers, tap on the forehead) with negative thinking. This trigger becomes associated with the negative thoughts and reminds the student to replace the negative thoughts with positive patterns.

THE POCKET PROCESS

The Pocket Process provides the student with a strategy for delaying thoughts that are interfering with attention and concentration on academic activities. Students are taught to put aside thoughts that are important but not relevant to the task at hand. This strategy should be taught when the interfering thoughts are low stress. The student may need to be cued to use the strategy for several trials before it becomes automatic.

STEPS

1. Identify the mentally distracting thought.

   Some examples might be:
   - Worrying about an up coming math test during English class.
   - Mentally replaying an argument.
   - Dreaming about summer vacation.

2. Write or draw the distracting thought on a piece of paper.

3. Fold the paper into a small square, put it in your pocket, and give yourself permission to think about it later.

4. Over time, replace the written thoughts with a mental process (bracketing):
   - Mentally put a fence around the intruding thoughts.
   - Walk through a gate.
   - Close the gate behind you.

CHAIRS IN PLACE

The Chairs in Place strategy provides students with a method for removing themselves from an area of high distraction to an area more appropriate to the task. It is especially useful when the tasks are not intrinsically motivating or when others are engaged in a variety of tasks resulting in increased noise and movement. Students may need to be cued to use this strategy frequently before they are able to use this independently. The associated strategies of Accepting Feedback and Responding to Persuasion may need to proceed this strategy.

STEPS

1. After choosing a task, stop and think about the best place in the room to focus and concentrate on that task.

2. Take your materials to that location and complete the task. (Sometimes it may be necessary to ask permission to move to the new location.)

3. Some optimal places might be:
   - With your back to the rest of the students
   - Near the teacher, parent, or coach
   - Away from doors, windows, and air conditioners (or other noisy places)
   - Near another student who shares your commitment to the task

4. After completing the task, compare the time needed in the new location with the time need in the old location.

THE THREE-FOLD PAGE

The Three-Fold Page (or 3-Fold Page) strategy gives the student a method of reviewing key information that is interactive and repetitive. With each repetition, the student comes closer to meeting the challenges of a summative evaluation and gains self-efficacy. This strategy combines identification of key information, memorization, and practice with retrieval, and requires students to identify the key information. A process for recognizing the key points may need to be mastered before the student can use this strategy independently.

STEPS

1. Fold a piece of notebook paper into three equal parts to form six columns (front and back).

2. Label each column alphabetically from A to F.

(front)			*(back)*		
A	**B**	**C**	**F**	**E**	**D**

3. Write the key words (the answers to test questions) in column A.

4. Fill in the key information (the test questions) in column B.

5. Fold under column A under so that only B and C show. From memory write the answers to the key information column C. Unfold column A and check your work. Do a math problem to determine your level of readiness.

6. Fold under column C and turn the paper to the back. From memory, write the key information about the key words in column D. Look at column B only after writing all the key information you can from memory. Do a math problem to determine your level of readiness.

7. Lay the page so that only the back shows. Write the key words for each item written in column E. Check your work against column A only after answering all the information you can from memory. Do a math problem to determine your level of readiness.

8. Fold under column D so that only column E and F can be seen. From memory, write the key information in column D. Look at column B only after writing all the key information you can from memory. Do a math problem to determine your level of readiness.

9. Identify any key words or information you are having a difficult time remembering, and prepare a separate three-fold page for them.

10. Repeat steps 3 through 8.

THE THREE-FOLD PAGE (BACK)

F	E	D

THE THREE-FOLD PAGE (FRONT)

A	B	C

CORNELL NOTES

The Cornell Method of note taking provides the student with a strategy for constructing for meaning by transacting with the text while recording information that is self-organized and concise. The Cornell Method enables the student to produce a polished set of notes that is both a record of the material assigned and a study and review guide.

STEPS

1. Date the top of the page and identify the subject and unit being studied.

2. Draw a line 3 inches from the left edge of the paper. (The page is divided into one-third and two-third segments.) Label the one-third column RECALL.

3. Write notes in the two-thirds segment of the page. Take brief notes using key words. Skip lines between main ideas. Leave spaces if an idea is missed or questions arise.

4. As soon as possible after class, read through the notes and fill in any blanks. Highlight the key words and ideas.

5. Fill in the recall column with key words, mnemonic devices, diagrams, or questions.

6. Draw a line across the paper one or two inches from the bottom and label this SUMMARY. Write a brief summary of the notes on this page in your own words.

7. Review the notes daily by folding the page so that only the RECALL column is showing. Repeat the review with only the Key Information Column showing.

EXAMPLE

Earth Science—Ocean Facts	10/15/98
Recall	**Key Information**
P I – AAA	5 oceans — Pacific, Indian, Atlantic, Antarctic, Arctic
Deepest?	Deepest — Atlantic
Largest?	
Summary	
Five oceans cover the earth. They are the Pacific, the Atlantic,…	

2-COLUMN NOTE TAKER

Name _____ Subject _____ Date _____

Key Term	Use a few high information words to define or explain the key term.
Summary	

STOP AND THINK

The Stop and Think strategy gives the student a metacognitive process to determine whether they understand a text while they are interacting with it. The Stop and Think strategy is an essential part of many other strategies and frameworks such as *Math Assault, Goal Setting, Muscle Reading,* and *The Objective Test-Taking Cycle.* It may need to be taught and mastered before proceeding to the more complex processes. This is an essential strategy for impulsive students who tend to work too quickly and for failure syndrome students who give up too easily. It is critical for students with low self-efficacy.

STEPS

1. Read a predetermined number of pages, study a picture, or math problem.

2. Stop reading or examining and ask:
   - Does this make sense to me?
   - Where have I seen (heard) of this before?
   - How is this like experiences (problems) I have had before in class (in life, seen in movies, etc.)?

3. Read on (examine more) and stop and think about the next section (or problem.)

Note: Students should be instructed in strategies to use if they do not understand the material or cannot relate the passage to their own experiences even though they have stopped and reflected.

MUSCLE READING

Muscle Reading provides a student with a three-phrase technique for extracting knowledge and information from extended passages in textbooks. A variation of *SQRRR*, this system works especially well for social studies and science texts where embedded language and dense information are the norm. At first, the multistep framework may seem awkward and cumbersome, and it does take time to learn and master. The payoff is less time rereading material and a well-constructed test-preparation study guide.

Phase I—Before you read (5 to 15 minutes depending on length of reading assignment)

1. Preview—Flip through the pages of the assigned reading. Notice section headings, read picture captions, and look at bold face words until you get to the end of the assigned reading. If there is a chapter review at the end of the reading, read it first. If a vocabulary list is included read those words and identify any that you already know. This step is a warm-up exercise, activating prior knowledge.

2. Outline—Notice how the reading is organized. Quickly read the section titles and paragraph headings. Decide whether a mind map, Post-Its, Cornell Notes, or a formal outline will be best to use during the reading and set up the note-taking format.

Phase II—Reading (10 to 30 minutes depending on length or difficulty of the assignment)

3. Read—Visualize the material. Read aloud when you feel your mind wandering. Reading aloud is especially good for complicated material. Sit up and avoid reading in bed except for fun.

4. Underline, highlight, write Post-Its or Cornell Notes, or fill in a mind map or outline as you read.

5. Answer—Write the answers to the questions in the section review, or study guides, or that you asked yourself during the prereading phase. Expand your outline, mind map, Post-Its, or Cornell Notes. Write down new questions as they occur to you. Think of yourself as a detective figuring out what will be on the next test.

Phase III—After you read (5 to 10 minutes depending on detail gleaned from the assignment)

6. Recite—Talk to yourself about what you have learned. Explain as much as you can about each key point you have listed.

7. Review—Within 24 hours of reading the material. Look at your notes, fill in anything that you don't understand, recite some of the main points. Check to see what is already in your memory.

8. Review again—Read your notes once a day for about 5 minutes. Recite the more complicated information.

Based on the work of Ellis, D. B. (1991). *Becoming a Master
Student.* Rapid City, SD: College Survival.

GRAPHIC ORGANIZERS[1]

Using Graphic Organizers provides the student with structures that organizes large amounts of information or abstract information into a graphic representation. A student can then use the information on the graphic organizer to prepare for tests, write essays, correct understanding, analyze information, draw conclusions, or make connections.

STEPS

1. The student selects an appropriate "blank" from an assortment provided by the instructor or creates a mind map using circles and connected lines.

2. The student gathers information and places the information onto the graphic organizer in appropriate boxes, columns, circles, etc.

3. The graphic organizer can then be used to prepare for tests, write essays, correct understanding, analyze information, draw conclusions, etc.

EXAMPLES

Function	*Graphic Organizers*
Constructing Knowledge	Semantic Maps including Webbs Debate Organizers
Clarifying/Connecting Details	Core Planning Charts Taba Charts Concept Clarifiers
Recognizing Patterns	Action-Reaction Charts Problem-Solving Structures Cause & Effect Diagrams
Elaborating	Multiparagraph Organizers Mind Maps

---

1 Two Excellent sources of Graphic Organizers are Black, H., & Black, S. (1990), *Book I and Book II—Organizing Thinking: Graphic Organizers,* Pacific Grove, CA: Midwest Publications, and Ellis, E. (1999), *Using Graphic Organizers to Make Sense of the Curriculum,* Tuscaloosa, AL: Masterminds.

MATH ASSAULT

A developing sense of self-efficacy can be undermined by course work that is out of alignment with a student's learning style or level of abstract reasoning. The Math Assault strategy gives a student a systematic, concrete process for solving high-level mathematics problems using both auditory and visual modes. This strategy enables an instructor to detect and correct errors in a student's problem-solving process and ends with a "paper memory" that a student can use in solving other abstract problems. Color-coding paper to organize topics or laminating the model sheets for permanent storage and reference is also useful.

STEPS

1. Write a problem on the top of a notebook page or 6" x 8" note card.

2. Verbalize and record the mathematical steps as you solve the problem.

3. Verbalize the steps again as you write the steps in sentence form beside each step.

4. Use the paper or card for reference when solving similar problems and when preparing for tests and quizzes, or as a cued note system during a test.

	Factor completely $x^2 - 8x + 15$ and check using FOIL
1. (x)(x)	1. x times itself is x^2 so I can write that in each parenthesis.
2. (x –)(x –)	2. The plus sign in front of the 15 tells me both signs will be the same. The minus sign in front of the 8x tells me both signs will be negative. I can write that in each parenthesis.
3. (x – 3)(x – 5)	3. What two numerals will multiply to the last numeral and add or subtract to the middle numeral? 1,3,5, and 15 are the multiples. Three and five add to eight and multiply to 15; I can write 3 and 5 in the parenthesis.
4. FOIL	4. Write the FOIL (First, Outside, Inside, Last) mnemonic under my solution.
5. x^2	5. The first two terms in each parenthesis means x times x. That is x^2.
6. –5x	6. The outside terms in each parenthesis are x times –5. That is –5x.
7. –3x	7. The inside terms are –3 times x. That is –3x.
8. +15	8. The last terms are –3 times –5. That is +15.
9. –5x and –3x are –8x	9. The only like terms are the middle two. –5x –3x combine to –8x.
10. x2 – 8x + 15	10. Write the complete expression and compare to the original problem.

REQUESTING HELP OR ACCOMMODATIONS

The Requesting Help process provides a strategy that allows students to seek assistance so they can cope with information, directions, assignments, and personal problems. Students can use the same basic steps to request their accommodations.

STEPS

1. Decide specifically what the problem is (or what accommodation is appropriate to be requested) and form it into a statement. Be sure to consider the following:
   - Who or what is causing the problem?
   - Why is the accommodation needed and appropriate?
   - What is the effect of the problem on the student's learning or on the student's ability to show what the student knows?

2. Decide whether help (accommodation) is necessary to solve the problem or whether the problem can be solved without help (accommodation).
   - A teacher should help students separate power plays and attention-seeking behaviors from requests for solutions. If the student's goal is to engage in a battle, help is inappropriate. Words such as win or lose, right or wrong, and fair should be avoided if possible.

3. (Optional step) Brainstorm to come up with a list of people who might help and pick one.
   - The teacher should encourage all possible helpers so that the student can choose the best one.

4. Rehearse stating the problem (or accommodation) defined in step 1, and practice asking specific questions.

5. If necessary, make an appointment with the helper chosen and ask that person for assistance.

6. Ask for help or an accommodation.

NOTEBOOK ORGANIZATION STRATEGY

The Notebook Organization Strategy provides the student with a routine to become orderly with his or her materials. The goal is to form the habit of routinely cleaning and filing. Students may need the teacher's assistance in deciding what materials need to be filed and what materials can be discarded.

STEPS

1. Establish the purpose for orderliness—help the student understand the relationship between organization of materials and success.

2. Clean locker, book bag, textbooks as follows:

   - Place all pens, pencils, rulers, calculators, erasers, etc., together in the front pocket of the book bag or in a plastic pouch in a three-ring binder.

   - Divide binder into separate sections for each subject, have a separate pocket folder for each subject, or have a separate spiral notebook for each subject.

   - Date all assignments, notes, worksheets, and place them into the separate subject areas at least once a week. Daily filing is recommended.

Note: Students who complete homework and then cannot find the work need to design a separate system of filing completed homework. These students might benefit from having a homework folder that is separate from the subject area work. That folder should have the completed homework in it and should be empty by the end of each school day.

ACCEPTING FEEDBACK

The Accepting Feedback process provides students with a strategy that enhances their ability to listen to feedback—both positive and negative—and to use that information to change or maintain behavior. If the student is unable to "hear" the feedback, an associated strategy such as *Responding to Persuasion* or *Following Instructions* may need to proceed this strategy.

STEPS

1. Listen carefully while you are receiving the feedback. Take notes, nod your head, or say "mm-hmm" so that the person giving the feedback knows you are listening.

2. Ask questions about anything that you don't understand so that the feedback is specific and clear. Do not argue with the feedback or try to defend and explain away the feedback.

3. Accept the positive feedback and acknowledge the compliment or recommendation.

4. Repeat any suggestions on how to change the negative feedback to positive feedback.

5. Decide what you think about the negative feedback by separating your ideas from the other person's ideas and say your ideas aloud.

6. Decide if you can follow the suggestions and let the other person know your decision.

7. Do what has been decided.

ELIMINATING OPTIONS

The Eliminating Options strategy provides the student with a decision-making guide to identify the distractors on a test. Students can find and cross off the distractors, focus on the remaining options, and improve their chances of a correct response. This strategy can also be used with any assigned work that requires choosing among many options and is an essential skill for students who have a tendency to perseverate. All students should be taught *Response Generation,* reading the stem of the multiple-choice question without looking at the options and trying to answer the question before looking at the options, as a companion strategy.

STEPS

1. After using *Response Generation,* read all the options and find the one that best matches your initial response. If your answer is not an option given on the test, use the following guidelines to eliminate the options:

    *   Cross off the answers that are obviously wrong.
    *   If two answers are similar, except for one or two words, choose one of these.
    *   If two quantities or dates are almost the same choose one of those.
    *   If two word choices sound similar (basalt, balsa) choose one of those.
    *   If dates cover a wide range (1052, 1492, 1865) choose the one in the middle.

2. Use *Steal It*—recognize and use names, dates, and places in other questions as clues to help answer more difficult questions.

3. Read the stem with each option to see which answer best fits or sounds the most familiar.

4. If all of the above strategies have failed, mark the question and leave it for later. (Sometimes the answer will "float" into working memory when ignored, or another question will trigger the answer.)

5. If there is no penalty for guessing and you still cannot answer the question when you return to it, close your eyes and pick an answer. You will be correct about 12 percent of the time.

MICOLUCCI'S TIME MANAGEMENT CHECKLIST

The Time Management Checklist strategy provides students with a process that allows them to record assignments and plan for task completion. *Assignment Tracking* and *Grade Tracking* are necessary companion strategies for the time management strategy to be most successful.

STEPS

1. The student, with the guidance of the teacher, brainstorms a list of critical steps for academic success.

2. The student or teacher types up the list in the form of a checklist and places the checklist in the assignment notebook (or another specific location).

3. The student uses the checklist daily to organize and plan his or her time.

EXAMPLE

Teacher	Subject	Checklist
Jones	Algebra I	☐ Completed all homework on time ☐ Accurately completed assignment book ☐ Practiced at a set time each day ☐ Identified up coming assignments ☐ Planned for completion of assignments ☐ Kept track of grades
Smith	9th English	☐ Completed all homework on time ☐ Accurately completed assignment book ☐ Asked someone to edit essays ☐ Identified up coming assignments ☐ Planned steps for long-term projects ☐ Kept track of grades

Contributed by George Micolucci, May 1999.

WOOMER'S HARD-TO-EASY METHOD OF PRIORITIZING

A prioritizing strategy provides the student with a decision-making routine that identifies the work that needs to be done first. This method is designed for students who routinely complete easy tasks first and avoid engaging in the more difficult tasks. The students need to have developed skill in recording a correct task list (see *Assignment Tracking*) before they can effectively set priorities.

STEPS

1. Create a daily list of all the work that you have been assigned.

2. Determine which items on the list are the most difficult. These are the tasks that will take a lot of time or require someone's help or explanation. Mark those with a capital H.

3. Determine which items are easy and can be done independently. These tasks are important but will not take very much time nor require someone's help or explanation. Mark those with a capital E.

4. Go back through your list and schedule time to complete all the H tasks when a helping person will be nearby.

5. As you complete each H task, cross it off your list. Then do one E task and cross it off.

6. At the end of the day, evaluate your performance:
    - Look for any H task you did not complete.
    - Look for assignments that repeatedly show up as H tasks and never get done.
    - Discuss with someone what causes these tasks to be ignored.
    - Identify the characteristics of the task that makes it difficult.

Contributed by Jon Woomer, May 1997.

GRADE TRACKING

The Grade Tracking strategy provides students with a way to record the grades that they earn. This strategy works especially well for students who have difficulty seeing the "big" picture, students who tend to remember only the good news, and students who only increase their effort during the last two weeks of a marking period. The strategy requires students to record grades as they receive them and to use that information to determine which courses need the most attention.

STEPS

1. Given a record sheet, establish a grade goal for each class and record that information.
2. At least once a day, record grades received by class in an assignment notebook or on a grade sheet.
3. Calculate the current grade in each class at regular intervals. Daily calculation may be needed for some students; others may need to calculate their current averages weekly.
4. Use the liaison report or a teacher conference to confirm the accuracy of the student's information at regular intervals.
5. Compare the current grade average to the goals and identify the subjects that are below the goal.
6. Form a Plan of Action for that course.
7. Repeat the process.

EXAMPLE

SUBJECT:			
TERM:	GOAL:		
TEACHER:			
DATE	ASSIGNMENT	GRADE	CURRENT AVERAGE

CONFERENCING

The Conferencing strategy provides the student with a strategy for inter-acting cooperatively with teachers, parents, and peers. Learning this process enables the student to gain and share information. When this strategy is learn-ed, it can be used to reinforce skills, to gain feedback on progress, to externalize thought processes, and to increase understanding—all essential components of self-efficacy. Conferencing can serve as a catalyst for the creation of new ideas, as well as encouraging reflection and revision. Students need to be proficient in *Accepting Feedback* and the use of positive self-talk such as the *I Can* strategy be-fore Conferencing can be used. Some associated strategies, such as *Responding to Persuasion* or *Following Instructions* may need to precede this strategy.

STEPS

1. Determine the purpose of the conference (discussion, problem solv-ing, training, tell back, feedback, progress report, etc.)

2. Listen carefully—takes notes, nod your head, or say "mm-hmm" so that the others in the conference know that you are listening.

3. Ask questions about anything that you do not understand. Do not argue or insist on your own way.

4. Using "I" messages that are empty of personal criticism, offer your ideas, opinions, or suggestions. Do not argue or insist on your own way.

5. Decide which ideas, information, suggestions you intend to use and let the other person know.

6. Keep a record of the conference.

FOLLOWING DIRECTIONS

The Following Directions strategy teaches students to comply with the teacher's classroom instructions or the requests of another person.

STEPS

1. Listen carefully without interrupting while the directions are being given. Take notes if necessary, make eye contact or say "mm-hmm" so that the other person knows that you are listening.

2. Ask questions about anything that you don't understand so that the instructions are specific and clear.

3. Repeat the instructions to yourself.

4. Do what you have been instructed to do.

DISTRIBUTED STUDY PROCESS

Distributed Study (as opposed to massed study) provides the student with a review routine that emphasizes the importance of learning material periodically throughout a unit of study. The reviews or "study" sessions are spread into daily reviews, weekly reviews, and major reviews. The major reviews occur a day or two before a major test and five days before an exam. However, the bulk of the memorization is done during the daily and weekly reviews, well before the test or exam.

STEPS

1. Daily reviews: (5 to 10 minutes)
   - Concentrate on memorizing material you have just learned.
   - Read or recite the material just presented in class.
   - Make flash cards, complete Cornell notes, etc., on that information.
   - Do a quick check on your memory of the information learned previously.

2. Weekly reviews: (30 to 45 minutes)
   - Check your memory for all information presented to date.
   - Separate information you know from the information still not in memory.
   - Use a memory strategy for the information still not in long-term memory.
   - Add any missing information to new flash cards, Cornell notes, etc.
   - Create a memory for each item.
   - Check your memory again.
   - Separate the facts that are in memory from those that are not yet stored.

3. Major reviews: (45 to 60 minutes, 2 days in a row before tests, 5 days in a row before exams)
   - Begin the review with the information that has been the most difficult for you to retain.
   - Check your memory for all facts—even those you are sure you have in long-term memory.
   - Separate information that does not leap to mind immediately.
   - Study for 20 minutes then take a short 5-minute break.
   - Create memories for the difficult information again.
   - Repeat this process until the hour is up or the information is easily retrieved.

COVER AND RECITE
(REHEARSAL AND RETRIEVAL PRACTICE)

The Cover and Recite strategy provides students who prefer to study alone with a method of checking their test readiness and to practice retrieving information from their memory. This method of covering, reciting, and checking works well as long as students do not fool themselves into believing information is in long-term memory when it is not. If a student does not know the answer when it is covered, but the response is familiar when uncovered, the information is not yet in long-term memory and needs to be rehearsed. It should be noted that this method of studying could be used for both rehearsal and retrieval, but must be done *ad nauseam*. This strategy differs from "going over" information, which is the most common method of studying as reported by students. If "going over" information was an excellent rehearsal strategy, grades on tests would be much better then they are.

STEPS

1. After deciding on a system of marking correct and incorrect answers, cover the answer and read the question you have prepared.

2. Answer the question and then reveal the correct response. Compare your response with the correct answer and note it in some way. (List right and wrong answers, stars and checks, two separate piles, etc.)

3. Choose a rehearsal strategy that matches your learning style, and use it to learn the information that you got wrong or did not know.

4. Repeat the process.

ORAL RETRIEVAL

Oral Retrieval is a process for checking test readiness using an auditory strategy. Students employ this method when they ask someone to quiz them. The vocalization of the information further reinforces memory. The purpose of Oral Retrieval is to decide readiness for testing or the need for further preparation. Care must be taken that the "testing pairs" switch roles. Testing pairs are most successful when they share common academic, not social, goals. Rehearsal and retrieval strategies should not be used simultaneously. Information that is not in long-term memory should be noted in some fashion, and a rehearsal strategy should be used at a later time.

STEPS

1. After deciding on a system of making correct and incorrect answers, give your list, graphic organizer, flip pack, flash cards on a ring to a study partner.

2. One study partner reads the question (or reveals the question in some way for a visual learner) and the other partner tries answering.

3. Correct, wrong, or unknown responses are noted in some way— lists, stars, checks, two separate piles, etc.

4. If both partners are taking the test, switch roles and repeat the process.

5. Choose a rehearsal strategy that matches your learning style, and use it to learn the items that you got wrong or did not know.

RESPONDING TO PERSUASION

The Responding to Persuasion process instructs the student in a strategy that promotes listening with an open mind and enables the student to separate ideas from personality.

STEPS

1. Listen to the other person's ideas on a topic without interrupting. Make eye contact or say "mm-hmm" so that the other person knows that you are listening.

2. Repeat the other person's ideas in your own words beginning with, "So, what you are telling me is...."

3. Decide what you think about the topic and say your ideas aloud.

4. Compare what the other person said with your ideas.

5. Decide one of the following things and share it with the other person:

   - I agree with your ideas because...
   - I disagree with your ideas because...
   - I would modify your idea this way...
   - I would like more time to think about your ideas I will get back to you on...

KEY WORD PICTURES

This rehearsal strategy uses substitution, imagery, association, and humor to remember information. It is used when large amounts of information need to be retained, or when a concept or fact cannot be easily pictured or associated with prior knowledge. This strategy has the added benefit of being appropriate for any style of learner. Visual learners can make the images bold and colorful, auditory learners can include sounds, and kinesthetic learners can include movement.

STEPS

1. Select a word that has no meaning for you or that you are having trouble retaining.

2. Associate the sound of the word or the look of the word with a vivid, silly, or strange image that is linked to the unknown word.

3. Practice using the image to recall the true meaning of the word or to recognize the true meaning of the word on a test.

EXAMPLES

To remember that John Kay invented the Flying Shuttle, picture a giant white "K" with huge angel wings flying through the blue sky.

To remember that a crab belongs to the crustacean family, picture a crab holding a huge crust of bread in its claw as it walks down the beach.

To remember that "roja" is red in Spanish, picture a huge red rose laughing: Ha, Ha.

GUIDELINES

1. Make the image large and exaggerated.

2. Make the image move, speak, or sing.

3. Make the image bizarre, silly, and unusual.

4. Make the image resonate with sounds similar to the word to be remembered.

SPLASHDOWN

The Splashdown technique is a memorization/rehearsal strategy that students can use during the test itself. As soon as students receive the test, information, such as formulas, associations, and lists, are written directly on the test and used for references during the test. The strategy must be consciously created during the rehearsal stages of the *Objective Test-Taking Cycle* and then used during the test. The students must intend to use this method, have identified what will be important to prepare as a splashdown, and to have practiced writing the information before the test.

STEPS

1. Determine what information will be helpful as a guide during a test (math formulas or steps, memory joggers and associations used, abbreviations, etc.) and write the information on notebook paper, index card, or a sticky note.

2. Practice writing the information quickly from short-term memory. This should take no more than one or two minutes.

3. Take the written splashdown with you to the test. Refer to it until the instructor tells you to put it away.

4. As soon as the test is handed out and before looking at the test questions, jot down as much of the splashdown as you remember.

5. Use the information on your splashdown as a reference as you take the test. Include more information in mini-splashdowns as they occur to you.

GOAL VISUALIZATION

The Goal Visualization strategy provides the students with a process of affirmation when they are working toward the achievement of personal goals. When students have established their own goals, they are more likely to hold themselves responsible for fulfilling those goals, and the goals become self-evaluative motivators. When building self-efficacy, have students periodically visualize themselves achieving those goals, especially when they are working toward difficult goals. The frequency with which Goal Visualization needs to be done varies from student to student.

STEPS

1. Retrieve a copy of the goal.
2. Sit comfortably in a chair with both feet flat on the floor with your hands in you lap.
3. Read the goal, breath deeply three times, and close your eyes.
4. Picture yourself achieving your goals.
5. Describe the positive payoff and the feelings associated with the goal achievement.

RELAX WITH BLACK

The Relax with Black strategy provides the student with a process for reducing stress during a high-stakes activity, such as an exam or test, or during anxiety-producing activities, such as a college or job interview. This strategy should be taught during a period of low stress. The student may need to be cued to use the strategy during several trials before it becomes automatic.

STEPS

1. Close eyes and take a cleansing breath.
2. Hold hands and arms in a relaxed position.
3. Clear the mind of all intruding thoughts by visualizing only a black surface.
4. Every time an interfering visual creeps onto the black surface, erase it.
5. Return to black.
6. Take a cleansing breath and open eyes.

STEAL IT

The Steal It strategy gives the student an increasing sense of control by using the instructions, assignment directions, and previous questions to produce the best possible test answers, compositions, and topic sentences. The process of increasing attention to cues, signals, and the environment heightens the sense of control and self-efficacy.

STEPS

1. Read the question or directions.
2. Use as many of the words and ideas from the directions and questions as possible when composing your topic sentence or your thesis statement.
3. Turn the question into a statement and use that as your first sentence in a paragraph or essay.
4. Use previous test questions or directions to answer other questions.
5. Use grammar cues and clues to choose the best possible answer.

POST-IT PROCESS

The Post-It Process provides students with a strategy for having main ideas, questions, examples, information, and supporting details readily accessible and near the appropriate passages of a school text. It is a concrete way for students to interact with a text without defacing the property. This strategy can be used in conjunction with any of the paraphrasing or comprehension frameworks such as *Math Assault, Muscle Reading, Graphic Organizers*, or memorization strategies such as *Key Word Pictures*.

STEPS

1. Read text silently or subvocally.
2. On a Post-It, paraphrase the main idea, definition, or steps in a process.

   or

   Write a question that needs to be clarified or explained.
3. Place the Post-It near the section of the text or slightly off the page to serve as a place marker.
4. Use the Post-It during class discussion or guided practice or as a reminder to ask for clarification of information.
5. Peel the Post-It off the text and use it in conjunction with the appropriate memorization or comprehension strategy.

ASSIGNMENT TRACKING

The Assignment Tracking strategy provides the student with a way to record the assignments that they have been given. This strategy works especially well for large tasks that seem overwhelming. Students who tend to put off tasks that cannot be done quickly and never experience the satisfaction of completing difficult work will find this helpful. The strategy requires students to break assignments into small manageable pieces, to distinguish between completed work and work that still needs to be done at home, and to set a schedule for completing the unfinished work.

STEPS

1. All daily assignments are recorded in an assignment notebook.

2. Any assignments that are not completed by the end of the school day are highlighted.

3. Any long-term assignments are divided into small subtasks. Then, working back from the due date, students set a schedule for completing the work.

GUIDING QUESTIONS

1. "What should you do the night before (due date) to have the (project) ready?" (This should be cosmetic "polishing"—*no* major work.)

2. "Back up one day. What do you need to have completed this night to have only polishing work tomorrow?" (This needs to be an editing process—correcting errors from some type of editing process or comparing work to a rubric.)

3. "Back up one day. To know what errors need to be corrected tomorrow, what needs to happen on this day?" (This step needs to include someone, other than the student, editing the work and checking the work against the teacher's criteria.)

4. And so on until present day... (Guide student in dividing the work into 30- to 90-minute chunks by asking "How long will that take you to complete?" at each step.)

5. As work progresses, the teacher should inquire about how well the students are keeping to the planned schedule.

6. Teachers should also teach students how to replan—how to change a schedule when tasks take more or less time than expected.

MATERIALS CHECKLIST STRATEGY

The Materials Checklist strategy provides the student with a systematic process of preparing to come to school, go to class, or leave school for home with all the materials necessary to successfully participate in class and to complete assigned work. The checklist should be customized for the individual student so that he or she can arrive at a task with all the necessary materials needed.

STEPS

1. The student, with the guidance of the teacher, brainstorms all the materials needed for a typical day at school.

2. The student or teacher types up the list in the form of a checklist and places the checklist in a location where the student will readily see it.

3. The student compares the checklist against the notebook or book bag before leaving school for home, home for school, or before class and fills in any missing materials.

EXAMPLE

Student: _____

Do I have the following in my book bag?

Two or more pencils	Folders for each subject
Eraser	My homework for each subject
Two or more pens	Spiral notebook for each subject
Notebook paper	Textbooks for each homework assignment
Phone # of my study partner	Assignment notebook

A variation of the Materials Checklist can be used to systematically check work for those students who rush, fail to notice details, or who repeatedly make the same errors.

Math Checklist

1. Did I copy the problem correctly?	5. Did I follow the order of operations?
2. Did I highlight the signs?	6. Did I answer the question?
3. Did I record my *Splashdown*?	7. Is my answer near my estimate?
4. Did I label my answer?	

ATTENTION TAPE PROCESS

The Attention Tape Process provides students with a method of monitoring and charting their attention while performing a task that requires interacting with a text, such as reading for understanding. This process is also useful for students who have Attention Deficit Disorder, when they are doing any task that is not intrinsically motivating and can be used in any academic discipline.

STEPS

1. Make a tape recording that is completely silent except for a sound at odd intervals. The recommended time-interval pattern for a 30-minute tape is 3, 4, 3, 5, 4, 2, 4, 3, and 2 minutes. The sound should be pleasant and not jarring.

2. The students are instructed to begin work as the tape begins.

3. Each time the students hear the sound, they ask, "Am I on task?" and record a yes or no on a simple score sheet.

At the end of the study period (no more than 30 minutes), students total the time they were on task.

During subsequent study times, the students attempt to improve their on-task behavior.

ATTENTION TAPE RECORD

Student _____

Date	Yes	No	Date	Yes	No	Date	Yes	No
3			3			3		
4			4			4		
3			3			3		
5			5			5		
4			4			4		
2			2			2		
4			4			4		
3			3			3		
2			2			2		
Total all yes			Total all yes			Total all yes		

Date	Yes	No	Date	Yes	No	Date	Yes	No
3			3			3		
4			4			4		
3			3			3		
5			5			5		
4			4			4		
2			2			2		
4			4			4		
3			3			3		
2			2			2		
Total all yes			Total all yes			Total all yes		

APPENDIX II

FORMS

ACCOMMODATIONS

Name _____   Date_____

Disability _____

My Academic Strengths	Successful Strategies

My Learning Needs	Successful Accommodations or Bypass Strategies

Explain how your learning styles and intelligence strength affect your learning:

ACCOMMODATIONS CHECKLIST

(Adapted from Thurlow, M. L., Elliott, J. L., Ysseldyke, J. E. (1998). *Testing Students with Disabilities: Practical Strategies for Complying with District and State Requirements*. Thousand Oaks, CA: Corwin Press.)

Use the following checklist as a starting point to identify appropriate accommodations by answering the following questions about the student.

PRESENTATION

Yes	No	
☐	☐	1. Makes errors when reading silently.
☐	☐	2. Makes reading errors that cause misinterpretations of test questions.
☐	☐	3. Needs clarification of instruction, questions to answer correctly.
☐	☐	4. Distracted or overstimulated by densely typed text.
☐	☐	5. Can read text independently if text is enlarged.
☐	☐	6. Needs questions, directions paraphrased, simplified, or reworded to respond correctly.
☐	☐	7. Needs key words in directions and texts highlighted to identify critical information.
☐	☐	8. Omits or ignores parts of text without visual prompts.
☐	☐	9. Other _____

RESPONSE

Yes	No	
☐	☐	1. Can answer or compose significantly better when using a scribe.
☐	☐	2. Makes errors in the transfer of information from text to worksheet to answer sheet.
☐	☐	3. Does significantly better when allowed to physically cross out and eliminate options.
☐	☐	4. Makes patterns with bubble sheet answers.
☐	☐	5. Has difficulty filling in bubble sheets.
☐	☐	6. Other _____

SETTING

Yes	No	
☐	☐	1. Cannot work independently in a content classroom.
☐	☐	2. Needs assistance to complete written tasks.
☐	☐	3. Distracts others during assessment procedures.
☐	☐	4. Is highly distracted by noise or movement.
☐	☐	5. Can work in content classroom with a noise or movement buffer.
☐	☐	6. Performs best in a small group.
☐	☐	7. Other _____

INSTRUCTIONAL

Yes	No	
☐	☐	1. Has a limited knowledge of organizational and study strategies.
☐	☐	2. Needs guided practice in using self-management strategies.
☐	☐	3. Needs cues and verbal prompts to use strategies.
☐	☐	4. Other _____

SCHEDULING

Yes	No	
☐	☐	1. Has significant difficulty completing tasks in the same length of time as peers.
☐	☐	2. Does significantly better on daily or weekly assessments.
☐	☐	3. Can only work continuously for minutes.
☐	☐	4. Can complete tasks well if provided with periodic breaks.
☐	☐	5. Has periods during the day when medication has dissipated.
☐	☐	6. Other _____

ASSISTIVE DEVICES

Yes   *No*

☐   ☐   1. Can respond independently only when provided with the following device:

     Yes   *No*

     ☐   ☐   Calculator

     ☐   ☐   Spell checker

     ☐   ☐   Manipulative

     ☐   ☐   Pencil grip

     ☐   ☐   Page turner

     ☐   ☐   Computer

     ☐   ☐   Adaptive furniture

     ☐   ☐   Text talker converter

     ☐   ☐   Speech synthesizer

     ☐   ☐   Amplification device

     ☐   ☐   Brailler

     ☐   ☐   Tape recorder

     ☐   ☐   Magnification device

     ☐   ☐   Dictionary

     ☐   ☐   Other _____

MOTIVATIONAL

Yes   *No*

☐   ☐   1. Needs on-task reminders to complete tasks.

☐   ☐   2. Needs verbal prompts to recall information.

☐   ☐   3. Needs encouragement to sustain effort

☐   ☐   4. Needs cues or prompts to begin tasks.

☐   ☐   5. Gets "stuck" and needs prompts to go forward.

☐   ☐   6. Needs prompts to complete tasks that are not perfect.

☐   ☐   7. Needs cues to slow down or go back to complete skipped or missed information.

☐   ☐   8. Needs homework book check for accuracy in order to complete assigned work.

☐   ☐   9. Needs long-term projects periodically checked to complete them on time.

☐   ☐   10. Other _____

ASSIGNMENT NOTEBOOK GRADING SHEET

Student _____

1st Marking Period

Contents	*week 1*	*week 2*	*week 3*	*week 4*	*week 5*	*week 6*	*week 7*	*week 8*
1. Dated at least one month ahead								
2. Assignments recorded								
3. Grades recorded								
4. Long-term projects broken down								
5. Test preparation broken down								
TOTALS								

2nd Marking Period

Contents	*week 1*	*week 2*	*week 3*	*week 4*	*week 5*	*week 6*	*week 7*	*week 8*
1. Dated at least one month ahead								
2. Assignments recorded								
3. Grades recorded								
4. Long-term projects broken down								
5. Test preparation broken down								
TOTALS								

3rd Marking Period

Contents	week 1	week 2	week 3	week 4	week 5	week 6	week 7	week 8
1. Dated at least one month ahead								
2. Assignments recorded								
3. Grades recorded								
4. Long-term projects broken down								
5. Test preparation broken down								
TOTALS								

4th Marking Period

Contents	week 1	week 2	week 3	week 4	week 5	week 6	week 7	week 8
1. Dated at least one month ahead								
2. Assignments recorded								
3. Grades recorded								
4. Long-term projects broken down								
5. Test preparation broken down								
TOTALS								

BRIDGING THE GAP—
FROM OBSTACLES TO SOLUTIONS

Name _____ Date _____

Goal:

Obstacle	Solution

Goal:

Obstacle	Solution

Goal:

Obstacle	Solution

CONFERENCE PLAN/REPORT

Before the meeting:		
Agenda	Meeting date/time/place	Participants
	Materials	
Teacher's Positive Theme	Teacher's Strategy/ Suggestion	

During the meeting:	
Parent's Needs/Goals	Parent's Problems
Minutes of the Meeting	
Decision	

After the meeting:		
Benefits	What is in the way?	
Next Action by Parent	Next Action by Student	Next Action by School

DIFFERENTIATING INSTRUCTION
WITH THE PYRAMID PLANNER

Teacher _____   Unit _____

Content (differentiated by R I P)	Activities (differentiated by R I P ?)

What SOME will learn:

_____
_____
_____
_____

What MOST students will learn:

Products
(differentiated by R I P ?)

_____
_____
_____
_____

What ALL students should learn:

Learning Strategies

_____
_____
_____
_____
_____
_____

Teaching Strategies _____

Assessment _____

EVIDENCE OF MASTERY

Teacher _____ Date _____ Class ____ Unit _____

Students	*Knowledge* Identify & recall of infor- mation	*Compre- hension* Organiza- tion & selection of fact or ideas	*Applica- tion* Uses facts, rules, principles	*Analysis* Separa- tion of whole into com- ponent parts	*Synthesis* Combina- tion of ideas to form a new whole	*Evalua- tion* Judges or decides based on identified criteria

Level of Mastery	*Method of Evaluation*
√ Has demonstrated proficiency of learner outcomes	P = performance assessment
+ In progress on learner outcomes	A = assignment
− Has not yet demonstrated proficiency of learner outcomes	O = observation
	% = test (percentage correct)

EXPECTATIONS

Name _____ Date _____

People have expectations that influence our behaviors. Often the expectations we have for ourselves come from the expectations that others have for us. These expectations influence our behaviors in both positive and negative ways.

Directions:

1. Identify three people in your life who hold expectations for you. Using magazines or personal drawings, find a picture or symbol of each person. Be sure to include yourself on the list.

2. Affix the pictures to a page in your Thinking Journal, and write an expectations statement that each would have of you.

3. Develop a response statement that each would have if you improved your self-efficacy skills, and write it below each picture.

4. Write a paragraph in your journal describing your feelings about meeting the expectations of the people in your life.

FROM STRENGTHS AND WEAKNESSES TO GOALS

Name _____ Date _____

Strengths—list at least four things you know and do that lead to school success	**Weaknesses**—list at least four things you do or habits you have that get in the way of school success

Goal-Setting Activity

Directions: Set three goals for the marking period. Each goal must be specific, clear, and challenging but attainable through your own efforts. Each goal must be something that is important to you and that you are willing to work toward achieving.

1. _____

2. _____

3. _____

Why are these goals important to you? _____

_____

_____

What will you need to do differently to achieve your goals? _____

_____

_____

GOAL-SETTING PYRAMID

Student _____ Date _____

One long-term
goal—Achievable by
the end of the school term

1. _____

_____

Two mid-term goals—Achievable by
the end of the current semester

1. _____

_____

2._____

_____

Three short-term goals—Achievable by the
end of the current marking period

1. _____

_____

2. _____

_____

3. _____

_____

1. These goals are important to me because _____

_____

2. My reward for achieving these goals will be _____

_____

3. I will share my goals with _____

_____

4. I will know I have achieved my goals when _____

_____

GOAL VISUALIZATION—
IMAGINE THE POSSIBILITIES

Name _____ Date _____

Directions: Often the language we use guides our behavior and shapes the possibilities we believe we have. In this exercise, you will hunt for any negative words that you are using as road blocks to your academic success and then relax and visualize yourself completing what *you* intend to accomplish.

1. List several academic goals you intended to achieve since school began.

   _____

   _____

   _____

2. Reread your list and highlight words like "hope," "try," "harder," "good," and "study." These words are vague or have very little specific, concrete meaning. They sound good, but do not identify any specific action or intention. Consider how you might sabotage your own intentions. You know yourself better than anyone does. How might you be causing your own failures?

   _____

   _____

   _____

3. Write what you intend to do between now and the end of the semester. Avoid writing in the negative (what you will not do) and avoid using the words from #2. State exactly what you intend to do and how you will know if you have done it. Make your intentions dependent on you alone.

   _____

   _____

   _____

4. Visualize yourself achieving your intentions. Think about one of the specific goals you have written. Sit comfortably in your chair and gently close your eyes. Imagine yourself completing the goal. Write an affirmation statement that says that you completed the goal you just visualized.

   _____

   _____

   _____

INTENTIONS—
WHERE DO WE GO FROM HERE?

Name _____ Date _____

Directions: Personal goal achievement is not easy especially if the goals you have set for yourself involve effort. Planning is required if you are to succeed. This evaluation will help you look at your progress thus far and help you decide if you are taking the steps necessary to achieve challenging goals.

1. Locate the goals you developed for this semester and reread the journal entries you made about your goals.

2. Prepare a journal entry using the following guidelines:
   - Put today's date on the top of the page and restate your short-term objectives.
   - Contrast your intended strategies (action plan) with what you actually did and write about activities or feelings that got in the way. Why did they get in the way? What will you need to do differently?
   - Write about what helped you. How are you feeling about your progress and the opportunities in the rest of the school year?

3. Write four specific actions you intend to take during the next marking period.

   I intend to _____

   _____

   I intend to _____

   _____

   I intend to _____

   _____

   I intend to _____

   _____

4. Give your journal and your intentions to the instructor for a response, and schedule a conference to explain your intentions.

THINKING SKILLS LIKERT SCALE

(Adapted from the Unionville High School Thinking Skills Project.)

Date _____ Grade _____ Subject _____   Teacher _____

Indicator*	Always (5)	Usually (4)	Some-times (3)	Occa-sionally (2)	Not Yet (1)	Not Ap-plicable (0)	Comments, Observations, Evidence
Perserverance	5	4	3	2	1	0	
Decreased impulsivity	5	4	3	2	1	0	
Flexibility	5	4	3	2	1	0	
Metacognition	5	4	3	2	1	0	
Careful review	5	4	3	2	1	0	
Problem posing	5	4	3	2	1	0	
Past knowledge	5	4	3	2	1	0	
Enjoyment of problem solving	5	4	3	2	1	0	
Precise language	5	4	3	2	1	0	

* See page 181 for definition, observable behaviors, and prompts for these indicators.

CHARACTERISTIC	DESCRIPTION	BEHAVIOR	CUES/PROMPTS
Perseverance	Working until solution is reached	Tries again, debates strategy, changes strategies	Look at this again. What else might you try?
Decreased impulsivity	Pausing to reflect or clarify, requesting more information	Asks for facts, pauses before answering	Speed doesn't count. Gather your thoughts. Take your time.
Flexibility	Considering the other points of view, trying new approaches	Paraphrases others, accepts suggestions or directions, evaluates responses	Can anyone think of another way to... Let's try looking at this another way.
Metacognition	Analyzing, describing one's own thought processes	Retraces steps, describes strategies and processes used	Go through the steps aloud. How did you do that?
Careful review	Proofing work, comparing work to criteria or exemplar	Reflects on accuracy of work, checks to ensure accuracy	Did you compare your work to the rubric? Have you used a peer editor?
Problem posing	Asking questions and finding problems to solve	Wonders. Asks for proof or evidence	How do you know? What would happen if...?
Past knowledge	Using prior knowledge or past learning	Makes connection to past experience, content or ideas	Does this remind you of anything else? Where else might this be useful?
Enjoyment of problem solving	Solving problems with increasing joy and independence	Positive comments. On task for extended period of time.	You're doing great. Keep working. I'm pleased to see you're hanging in there.
Precise language	Using appropriate descriptive words and labels	Uses analogies, complete sentences. Concise.	Stop and think first. What is the scientific word for that?

LONG-TERM PROJECT GOAL SETTING

Name _____ Date _____

Directions: Follow the six steps below to identify your science fair goals and to visualize your self completing what you intend to accomplish.

1. In your _____ journal, write your goal for the _____ project.

   - Be positive about what you intend to do and be willing to take a risk.
   - Challenge yourself but be realistic—give yourself the opportunity to succeed.
   - Break your largest goal into a series of smaller goals—What is your goal for this week? And for next week?

2. Break your goal into a series of intention—What you intend to do between now and the due date to achieve your goal.

   - Avoid writing in the negative—don't tell what you will not do.
   - Leave out words like "hope," "try," "harder," or "good."
   - Be specific about what you intend to do—What will it look like?

3. Set deadlines for each of your intentions and record each step in your assignment notebook.

4. Consider how you might sabotage your own intentions.

   - Have you made your goals dependent on you alone?
   - How might you cause your own failure?
   - What are the chances of you achieving your goals?

5. Relax, close your eyes, and picture yourself completing what you intended to accomplish.

   - Notice how you feel.

6. Write a goal affirmation sentence in your journal.

MUSCLE-READING BOOKMARK

MUSCLE-READING BOOKMARK

Phase I—POP

Preview (*look*)—pictures, chapter review, vocabulary list

Outline (*choose one*)—highlight, Post-It's, Cornell notes, list, flash cards

Pose Questions (*think*)—headings, bold words, section headings, homework

Phase II—RAP

Read (*slowly*)—visualize, recite, slow down, request help

Accent (*write as you go*)

Puzzle (*check and fill in*)—answer the questions

Phase III—ROAR

Recall (*explain all you know*)

Review (*memorize*)—key word pictures, do and redo, walk about, cover and recite

Review (*memory check*)

Repeat (*do Phase III again*)

MUSCLE-READING BOOKMARK

Phase I—POP

Preview (*look*)—pictures, chapter review, vocabulary list

Outline (*choose one*)—highlight, Post-It's, Cornell notes, list, flash cards

Pose Questions (*think*)—headings, bold words, section headings, homework

Phase II—RAP

Read (*slowly*)—visualize, recite, slow down, request help

Accent (*write as you go*)

Puzzle (*check and fill in*)—answer the questions

Phase III—ROAR

Recall (*explain all you know*)

Review (*memorize*)—key word pictures, do and redo, walk about, cover and recite

Review (*memory check*)

Repeat (*do Phase III again*)

OBJECTIVE TEST-TAKING CYCLE

Steps	Possible Strategies			Personal Plan
1. Set Goal: target a grade establish a time frame commit to strategies	Conferencing	Journalizing	Pyramid	
2. Identify the key information	Graphic Organizer Clustering Math Attack Color Coding	Cued Notes Highlighting Flash cards Skimming	3-Fold Page Cornell Notes Post-It's Muscle Reading	
3. Memorize the information	Walk About Do & Redo Acronyms Oral Rehearsal	Study Partner Peer Teacher Splashdown 3-Fold Page	Overlearning Write/Read Key Word Pictures	
4. Check memory	Practice Test Oral Retrieval Walk About	Study Partner 3-Fold Page Flash cards	Cover & Recite Splashdown Computer drill	
5. Adjust target grade	Reward Yourself	Goal Setting	Accepting Feedback	
6. Repeat Steps 3 to 5	I will repeat: 1 2 3 4 5 times			
7. Take test	Visualizations Eliminate Options Peek-a-boo Using Margins	Splashdown Steal It Triage Easy to Hard	Oral Retrieval Cued Notes SCORER Fore/Back	
8. Critique test performance	Reward Yourself Requesting Help	Conclusions Consequences	Skill Evaluation	
9. Adjust Strategies	Responding to Persuasion Decision Making		Responding to Help Requesting Help	
Repeat the cycle				

OBJECTIVE TEST-TAKING PLANNER

Name _____ Date _____

Step	*Strategies*
1. Set goal	1. What grade are you willing to work for?
2. Identify key information	2. How will you separate out the facts that will be on the test?
3. Memorize information	3. How will you get the information into long-term memory?
4. Check memory	4. How will you find out the facts are really in your memory and you can get them out of memory?
5. Adjust target grade	5. How will you know if you are as prepared as you wish to be?
6. Repeat Steps 3 to 5	6. How many times will you repeat Steps 3, 4, and 5 before the test?
7. Take test	7. What strategies will you use during the test?
8. Critique performance	8. How will you figure out what went right and what went wrong?
9. Adjust strategies	9. How will you prepare for the next test?

Repeat the Cycle

QUESTIONS TO ASK

Questions to ask students before the task

1. What do you think this lesson is about?

2. What are you to do in the lesson? Can you show me? Can you tell me?

3. Do you think you can do the task? If not, why not?

4. What do you already know about the topic?

Questions to ask student during the task

1. Tell me or show me what you are doing.

2. If you are unsure of what to do, how do you get help?

3. Talk to me about what you are learning.

4. What do you do when you do not understand something?

5. Is what you are doing easy or hard? Why?

Questions to ask students after the task

1. What did you learn from the lesson? about this topic?

2. Did you correctly predict what the lesson would be about?

3. What helped you to understand the lesson or topic?

4. How will you remember what you have learned?

5. How will you use what you have learned?

Adapted from Gickling, E. (1994). *Preparation for Adult Life*,
Secondary Instructional Support Assessment Workshop.
Chester County Intermediate Unit, Exton, PA, Nov. 1997.

REFLECTION—AM I WHERE I WANT TO BE?

Directions: Read your marking period goals and the strategies you chose to meet those goals. Then use the following questions to guide your preparation for a journal entry.

1. Did you achieve the short-term goals you established for this marking period?

2. What was harder than you expected?

3. What was difficult for you? What excuses did you use to avoid working toward your goals?

4. What did you find most encouraging or helpful?

5. Are you using your strategies regularly? Are they making a difference in your school success?

6. Do you still need to strengthen any strategy categories?

7. Are you as successful as you want to be?

Prepare a journal entry for each of the following questions:

PROGRESS: Have you reached your goals? Why or why not?

FACILITATOR: What is in the way or has slowed you down when you tried to reach your goal?

GROWTH: What did you learn during the marking period that you can use during the next marking period? What skills have you improved since the beginning of this year?

INTENTIONS: What will you do differently from now until the end of this school year so that you can reach the goals that you have set for yourself?

CHANGES: Do you need to change your goals or pick new strategies? Why or why not?

Give your journal to the instructor for a response.

SCORED DISCUSSIONS TALLY SHEET

Student →											
Offers position on topic (1)											
Makes a relevant comment (1)											
Uses evidence to support position (3)											
Points out contradictions (2)											
Recognizes irrelevant comments (2)											
Develops analogy (3)											
Asks a clarifying question (1)											
Uses active listening (3)											
Does not pay attention (–1)											
Distracting noises (–2)											
Distracting movements (–1)											
Interrupting (–2)											
Inappropriate humor (–2)											
Monopolizing (–3)											
Personal attacks (–3)											
Irrelevant comments (–1)											
Totals											

SEMESTER EVALUATION

Name _____ Date _____

Directions: Rate each academic area and explain any that are lower than they should be. Give your evaluation to the instructor for feedback and suggestions.

Academic Areas to Consider	Rating	Explanation	Teacher Suggestions
Report Card Grades			
Meeting Deadlines—homework, projects, test preparation			
On Time—to school, to class			
Self-assigned Homework— editing writing, test preparation, perfecting projects, practicing math			
Self-efficacy—knowing and using accommodations, learning style, strategies, accepting feedback, prioritizing			
Goal Attainment—daily, short-term, mid-term, long-term			
Time on Academic Tasks—in school, after school			
Keeping Track—homework, projects, test preparation, materials, grades			

Mastered: I do this automatically. This is part of my school behavior. No one has to remind me.

Good: I know how to do this, but I sometimes have to be reminded. Even though I know this will help me be more successful, I don't do this automatically.

Needs Work: I know I should do this, but I often need to be reminded. I only do this when an adult suggests this or reminds me it needs to be done.

Not Yet: I only do this when I am forced to or when I am being observed.

SETTING AND REFLECTING ON GOALS

1. Self-questioning by _____ Date _____
   - What are some good things that might happen to me if I improve my school performance?
   - What are some bad things that might happen to me if I improve my school performance?
   - What could keep me from improving my school performance?
   - Who can help me improve my school performance?

2. Goal Setting—Each goal must be specific, clear, and challenging but attainable through your own efforts. Each goal much be something that is important to you and that you are willing to work toward achieving.
   - As a short-term goal, I will _____
     _____
     _____
   - As a mid-term goal, I will _____
     _____
     _____
   - As a long-term goal, I will _____
     _____
     _____

3. Affirmation
   - Share your goals with someone you identified as helping you to improve.
   - Explain how you will achieve your goals and what the reward will be.
   - Arrange to meet regularly with the person to discuss your progress.

4. Reflection (think about these things after the meeting with your support person)
   - Were you satisfied with your progress?
   - Were your goals clear and sharp in your mind?
   - Did the support person you used keep you focused and honest?

SKILLS EVALUATION

(The following material continues on the next page.)

Student √ the box that is true of you			Name _____ Date _____	Teacher √ the box that is true of this student		
Mastered	Needs Work	Not Yet		Mastered	Needs Work	Not Yet
			Openness to Instruction			
			Uses suggestions given by teachers			
			Accepts skill instruction from teachers			
			Follows directions given by teacher			
			Quiets self, allows teacher to quiet			
			Asks for instruction and feedback to improve			
			Keeping Track			
			Homework (dates due, location)			
			Projects (dates, steps, rubric)			
			Test preparation (when, how often)			
			Materials (homework, textbooks, pens)			
			Strategy Repertoire			
			Has a variety of ways to study and learn			
			Can explain how to study and work			
			Chooses strategies that match learning style			
			Knows if a strategy is working well			

			Self-Efficacy/Determination/Advocacy			
			Asks for accommodations			
			Knows learning style			
			Knows personal strengths, weaknesses			
			Does the most important work first			
			Sets goals			
			Achieves goals			
			Self-Assigned Work			
			Test preparation			
			Projects			
			Writing, editing, rewriting			
			Organizing notebooks, locker, desk			
			Drill and practice			
			Time Management			
			Uses school time for completing work			
			Has a study routine for after school			
			Arrives on time to school			
			Arrives on time to class			
			Plans time for projects' deadlines			
			Plans time for test preparation			

SKILL EVALUATION CHECKLIST

Requests instruction for difficult work	Uses suggestions given by teacher	Quiets self or allows the teacher to quiet	Accepts feedback from teachers, peers	Has a variety of strategies to choose from	Chooses strategies that match problem	Learns new strategies	Works toward achieving goal	Date _____ Teacher _____ **Students**

M = Mastered	Student does this automatically. This is part of the student's school habits. No one has to remind the student to do this.
G = Good	Student can do this but sometimes needs to be reminded. Not an automatic part of this student's behavior.
W = Needs Work	Student knows how to do this but almost always needs someone to remind him or her.
Y = Not Yet	Student cannot do this or refuses to do this.

SMOKE AND MIRRORS

Directions: The process of writing down goals and making them public through an affirmation process dissipates the "smoke" and provides a "mirror" through which you can reflect on your progress.

1. Self-questioning by _____ Date _____
    - What are some good things that might happen to me if I improve my school performance?
    - What are some bad things that might happen to me if I improve my school performance?
    - What could keep me from improving my school performance?
    - Who can help me improve my school performance?

    _____

    _____

    _____

2. Goal Setting—Each goal must be specific, clear, and challenging but attainable through your own efforts. Each goal must be something that is important to you and that you are willing to work toward achieving.
    - As a short-term goal, I will _____
    - As a mid-term goal, I will _____
    - As a long-term goal, I will _____

3. Affirmation
    - Share your goals with someone you identified as helping you to improve.
    - Explain how you will achieve your goals and what the reward will be.
    - Arrange to meet regularly with the person to discuss your progress.
    - My meeting time with my support person will be _____

4. Reflection (think about these things after the meeting with your support person)
    - Were you satisfied with your progress?
    - Were your goals clear and sharp in your mind?
    - Did the support person you used keep you focused and honest?

    _____

    _____

STRATEGIES I NEED!

Student _____ Date _____

Directions: Pick your three most successful strategies, tell why you use it, and then think of a new use for the strategy.

Strategy #1 _____ **I need this because**	**I will use this for**

Strategy #2 _____ **I need this because**	**I will use this for**

Strategy #3 _____ **I need this because**	**I will use this for**

STRATEGIES THAT WORK!

Student _____ Date _____

Directions: Pick your three most successful strategies, tell why you use it, and then think of a new use for the strategy.

Strategy #1 _____	**Other uses:**
I used this for:	

Strategy #2 _____	**Other uses:**
I used this for:	

Strategy #3 _____	**Other uses:**
I used this for:	

STRATEGIES CRITICAL FOR SUCCESS

Name _____	Date _____
Directions: Highlight the strategies that you are currently using.	**Directions:** Describe how the strategy is contributing to your academic success.
Self-efficacy and Advocacy — Goal setting/achievement Goal Visualization I Can Accepting Feedback Requesting Help Management Checklists Test Critique	
Memorizing — Key Word Pictures Highlighting Oral Rehearsal Oral/Visual Retrieval Study Partner Cover and Recite 3-Fold Page Do & Redo	
Test Taking — Steal It Splashdown Eliminating Options Math Checklist	
Concentrating — Bracketing/Pocketing Chairs in Place Relax with Black Hard-to-Easy Easy First Distributive Study	
Composing — Graphic Organizers Steal It Oral Rehearsal Stop & Think Editing Partner Semantic Mapping	
Understanding — Post-It Process Stop & Think Cornell Note Taking Math Assault Muscle Reading	
Organizing — Assignment Tracking Grade Tracking Hard-to-Easy Prioritizing Materials Checklist Highlighting	

STUDENT SELF-CRITIQUE

Name _____ Date _____

Directions: Complete the critique below and attach to your completed project.

1. I was on the right track with my strategies for planning and completing my project, but what I didn't know was _____

    _____

2. I wish I had known more about _____

    _____

    _____

3. Three things I want you to notice about my project are:

    • _____

    • _____

    • _____

STUDY PLANNER

(The following material continues on the next page.)

Name _____ Date _____ Period _____ Teacher _____

THE HABITS

1. I **organize** myself during the first 5 minutes by making a 40-minute lesson plan that clearly identifies my goals, subjects, assignments, and strategies. I ask someone for assistance if I am unsure of what I need to accomplish.

2. I take responsibility for my **materials** by having all the supplies I need to complete the work I plan.

3. I show **commitment** by working the entire period, asking someone for assistance when I need information or instruction to complete my planned work.

4. I actively participate in my own education by **completing** the work I planned so that I can achieve the goals I have established.

5. I work **independently** but follow the teacher's suggested strategies, frameworks, and processes to improve my self-efficacy habits.

6. I quiet myself and put myself back **on task** or I allow others to put me back on task when I am unable to do so.

7. I **communicate** in an appropriate, confident, polite, clear manner.

THE PLAN

Goal:

_____

Subject: Subject:

_____   _____

Assignment: Assignment:

_____   _____

Strategy: Strategy:

_____   _____

THE SCORE

4 = Mastered   I do this automatically. This is part of my school behavior. No one has to remind me.

3 = Good	I know how to do this, but I sometimes have to be reminded. Even though I know this will help me be more successful, I don't do this automatically.
2 = Needs Work	I know I should do this, but I often need to be reminded. I only do this when an adult suggests this or reminds me it needs to be done.
1 = Not Yet	I only do this when I am forced to or when I am being observed.
0 = Not Ever	I refuse to do this or I do not think this is necessary for me.

	Student	*Teacher*	*Comments:*
1. Organize	_____	_____	_____
2. Materials	_____	_____	_____
3. Commitment	_____	_____	_____
4. Completing	_____	_____	_____
5. Independently	_____	_____	_____
6. On Task	_____	_____	_____
7. Communicate	_____	_____	_____
Total:	_____ +	_____	÷56 = _____%

TEST-TAKING CRITIQUE

Directions: Use this checklist to help identify the obstacles to achieving the grade you want on a test. Draw some conclusions from the analysis and then brainstorm some possible solutions.

Name _____   Subject _____

Test Date _____   Critique Date _____

Predicted Grade _____ Actual Grade _____   Next Target Grade _____

(✖) *Analysis*	(✍) *Conclusions/Possible Solutions*
_____ I should have started to prepare sooner than I did.	_____
_____ I did not schedule enough time for preparation.	_____
_____ I did the teacher-assigned homework and though my preparation was adequate.	_____
_____ I should have prepared a splashdown.	_____
_____ I should have picked a different strategy for preparation.	_____
_____ I prepared for recognition when I needed recall.	_____
_____ I was overconfident.	_____
_____ I studied the wrong information.	_____
_____ I had trouble understanding the questions or instructions.	_____
_____ I had trouble with the format of the test.	_____
_____ I misinterpreted what some of the questions were asking.	_____
_____ I made careless mistakes.	_____
_____ I ran out of time.	_____
_____ I guessed too much.	_____
_____ I choked or "blanked out" during the test.	_____
_____ I was unfamiliar with parts of the test.	_____
_____ I remember seeing the materials but could not "pull" the information from my memory.	_____
_____ Other _____	_____

THINKING JOURNAL PROMPTS

The _____ goal I was most focused on this week was…
      (subject)

It was hard for me to stay focused on my goals because…

As I worked toward achieving my goals, I was surprised to learn…

The strategy that brought me closer to my goals was…

It was more difficult than I thought it would be to…

After I set my goals, it was hard for me to…

My goal for next week is…

As I worked toward my goals, the most encouraging thing for me was…

I discovered the excuse I use to avoid working toward my goal is…

Before I set up my plan, I wish I had been told more about…

My goal for next week is to plan…

I organized all of my materials for class by…

This week was special for me because I am getting better at planning for…

I had some trouble planning for _____, but I solved it by…

I was surprised to learn that planning helped me to…

It was hard for me to learn…

Three strategies that I used today are…

This week I wished I had a better strategy for…

THE WEEK IN REVIEW

Date _____

This week I feel good about _____

_____

because _____.

_____

This week was easy for me because _____

_____.

I really had to put effort into _____

_____.

I had fun when _____

_____.

My goal next week is to _____

_____

_____

_____.

Signed,

_____

THE YEAR IN REVIEW

Date _____

This year I feel good about _____

_____

_____ because _____

_____ .

This year, I learned _____

_____

_____ and next year I intend to _____

_____ .

This year, the strategies that I used most successfully were _____

_____

_____

_____ .

The amount of academic support I will need next year is _____

_____

_____ because _____

_____ .

Signed,

_____

DATE DUE